Five Figure Funnels

How To Sell Marketing Funnel Services To Your Customers For Five
Figures In Any Market, No Matter Your Experience Michael Killen Sell
Your Service

Michael Killen

DEDICATION

For Chris, who taught me the first and last words in sales.

CONTENTS

ACKNOWLEDGMENTS

First of all I'd like to thank you for picking this book up. In retrospect it's really the first book I should have published and I'm glad it's being published now as I'm clearer than ever on the methodology within. I'd also like to thank my Friday accountability group for the support and advice while writing the book, and to my Mum for again being the first line of defence against my spelling. Thanks to Olivia for putting up with my long nights and loud dictation sessions and finally, I want to thank my good friend Dave Foy for the awesome foreword and trusting that I'd keep the content the same after he sent such kind words ;)

FOREWARD
by Dave Foy

I wish I'd known Mike Killen years ago. It's the 1990s and I'm a primary school teacher here in the UK. I adore teaching and the kids are great. But I despise what the government are doing to our education system. So after 10 years in the classroom, I quit. I start my new web design business with the following statement of intent:

"I ain't getting into that sales and marketing stuff. I just wanna build websites!" Bless my past naive self. Looking back 20 years ago, I'm not sure how I expected to get any work at all. My strategy consisted of praying for referrals while crossing my fingers. And while I did win new projects, each one was hard-won, one-by-one, a grind. My profits were wafer-thin to show for it. And still, I ignored marketing my web design business for many years. After all, marketing's for special marketing-minded people, with special marketing brains, saying special marketing words in the right order at the right time, right? All the sales and marketing training out there at the time seemed like a lot of snake-oil bullshit to me.

Thus the hoping and praying and scraping by continued. No system for attracting new clients. No clue how to price projects higher than mid-4-figures. More than once, it crossed my mind to throw in the towel and get a (whisper it) J-O-B. I loved my work. But the fact is, I already had a job. I didn't have a real business. I had a job. And one with crappy terms and a pretty clueless boss.

Ok, my time-travelling friend. Fast-forward. It's ten years ago, and I've joined forces with a good friend who actually enjoys this marketing stuff. I have almost no idea what he's talking about half the time. But he's super-enthusiastic about funnels and lead magnets and marketing automation and drinking copious amounts of tea. Together, we learn how to build and deliver marketing funnels. We test our ideas. We roll this stuff out on client projects. We get some really great results and wow, this shit works! We can prove ROI to new clients, baby! Boom.

1

So were we now profitable? No, we were not. Dammit. We were doing what we thought was right, of course. Believe me, effort and enthusiasm and good intentions were in plentiful supply. But like I say—I wish I'd known Mike Killen back then. I wish I'd had the book that you hold in your hands right now, you lucky thing. Because if I had, it would have saved me some serious facepalm action right now.

Yep, we cast the net nice and wide, building funnels for anyone and everyone who asked...We had no process—either for attracting new customers or delivering our service to them...We devised a bespoke solution for each unique snowflake of a business we worked for...We offered every possible service we could...We made several botched (though well-meaning) attempts to niche down, based on industries...Our enticing offer was the promise of "more leads and sales online" (I mean, who doesn't want that?!)...We thought it imperative to tell prospective clients about what we do...We set our prices "after" deciding what we were selling...(Do you recognise a bit of this yourself?)Our funnels delivered great ROI. Our clients' results were impressive. In fact, our clients were delighted. And us? We were exhausted, disheartened, and only sometimes profitable. We sure knew how to get results for our clients. But we hadn't cracked the code of how to sell our service. Four years ago I returned to my first love, teaching. I now teach non-coders how to build effective websites and marketing funnels with WordPress and Elementor. It's a multi 6-figures a year business, grown from the ground up with the same funnel strategies I learned in our agency.

Here's a question I hear often: "Great! I now know exactly how to plan, design, build and manage effective sales funnels. Dave, you're the man!" (alright, humour me) "Now tell me: how on earth do I sell these funnels to clients??" I know my limits. I'm sure you'll appreciate by now, I'm hardly qualified to answer this question. Enter Mike Killen. Mike is a force of nature. I'd heard OF him before I ever actually heard him or saw him. He was everywhere—podcasts, live streams, guest interviews. Friends frequently recommended I check him out. His bio said he was, "The world's #1 sales coach for funnel builders." Umm, really? He was saying you should be selling funnels for $25k and up. Yeah, right! I binge-watched his YouTube channel. I signed up for his email newsletter. I looked forward to his weekly podcast on my lunchtime walks. What he was saying made a ton of sense, all the exact opposite of "established wisdom".

I asked Mike if he'd deliver a workshop to my private student group, on how to sell marketing funnels. The workshop was, "How To Charge Five Figures For a Funnel". And in that workshop, he dismantled every belief and misconception my students had about selling their funnel service for $25k, or more. If only they had the right tech, the cleverest chatbot, the right experience, the right portfolio, the most complex funnels... No, no, no, no, no! That workshop became the most-watched bonus training in the course, by far. Several students put Mike's training into practice and won their first five-figure funnel projects. The advice, strategy and mindset changes he taught were absolute gold. And yet... that one hour workshop was but a fraction of the goldmine you're about to discover in this book.

I've since got to know Mike well and am lucky to count him as a valued mentor and good friend. I've had several coaching calls of my own with him. I've attended many training sessions in his brilliant Facebook group. I've watched him raise the roof at live events—if you get the chance to see Mike speak at an event, please take it. I've spent time with him, hanging out and shooting the shit. And yes, in case you're wondering, he does walk the walk, he does sell five-figure funnels. He's done what he's telling you to do in this book, over and over again. You'll be hard-pressed to find a more knowledgeable, generous and supportive coach.

Mike Killen has a way of making you see the world in a new way. He has a way of making you think more deeply, of thinking differently. He has a gift for dismantling the limiting beliefs that are blocking your progress. No, you do not need a bit more information, or some fancier tech, or more experience before you can charge five figures for a funnel. What you need is a tectonic mindset shift and to take the right action. So I'm excited for you! You're at the start of your journey towards marketing and selling your funnel services in a whole new way. Most books are more 'what to do', less 'how to do it'. Five Figure Funnels is most definitely all about exactly HOW. How to decide on your niche. How to price. How to sell. How to get referrals. How to find new customers. How to book calls and qualify leads for the customers YOU want to work with. How to write a proposal. Mike takes you step-by-step through every part of the process. Every step is action.

And take the steps you must. No-one's pretending that building your dream funnel business won't take hard work. So will you do me a favour? Don't waste this opportunity. Follow the steps. Take action. Please, don't look back in 12 months' time to find your life and business are exactly the same because you didn't put in the work laid out for you here. As Mike says:

"The profit and riches weren't in the mountain;
they weren't in the niche; they were in the steps you
carved into the side of the mountain."

Go climb that mountain. Carve your steps into it. I cannot wait to see you get to do what you love, make a difference in the world, and choose the life and business you want. My friend, your journey starts right here.
Dave Foy

INTRODUCTION

*"I can get started today, I just need a signature
and a deposit. I can even take payment today on my
phone."*

Those were the last words out of my mouth, finishing a short pitch to a media business that ran a few small TV stations and focused on daytime wellness and health shows. It was a £33,000 contract and the largest single proposal I had put together at the time. I was sweating and shaking as I said those words. And the silence afterwards was excruciating. Listening back to the recording it was only 2 seconds, but it felt like 20. During the silence I wanted to quit. I wanted to back out the room or shout out "ha ha! Joking! Obviously I wouldn't charge that kind of money. Who am I to demand such high fees?! I don't deserve this project, you'd be better off with someone else. I'm sorry I wasted your time."

My imposter syndrome was screaming at me internally. "Mike! Seriously, this isn't funny! They aren't going to fall for this!" I thought that I was going to be sick, all over the desk and the customer.

The deposit I talked about was £10,000 and would start the project. It included workshops, a small site build and some email marketing. I was 100% positive that they'd laugh at me, point to the door and tell me to get out. "Mike, that sounds perfect. Jim can you get the corporate card please? Let's get this going." Nick looked at me with a beaming smile. He had his hand outstretched ready to shake and I leant in to respond.

Holy cow. I did it. Nick continued to talk about how excited they were to start. Jim bought the card over and they entered the details. On my laptop they signed the contract and just like that, I was £10,000 richer, had a new project to give to my team AND I was excited to start. What had happened?

This book is designed to take you up to this point. The very scenario I start with here, is what you'll end up with by the time you finish. This book

4

is entirely focused on helping you sell a marketing funnel for five figures. You might feel as sick or heady as I did, when you ask for the deal. Or you might smash this out of the park and take it in your stride. I can't promise it'll always end in a "yes", but I can promise that you'll start finding more of the opportunities and landing them.

Before I went to this meeting, I had 3 bullet points in mind.
- Close them in the meeting and repeat the close
- Keep smiling
- Don't fill the silence

I was taught these by a mentor and he said to me that "as long as I remember to smile, don't try to fill the silence and repeat the close, you'll give it the best shot you can." After I closed my agency and moved onto Sell Your Service, I was at an event talking to marketers, funnel builders and agencies and the #1 question I was asked was "how can I sell a project for £10,000?" I would talk about niching and pricing and offer a few insights, but nothing really solid. There didn't seem to be a process or a system that I could explain to someone.

Years later I was at a seminar learning from Daniel Priestley (author of Key Person of Influence, Oversubscribed and others) on how to write and publish a book. I was learning from someone I very much admire and who themselves had multiple books and products and software. He asked us to write down the #1 question our audience asks us.

"How can I sell a marketing funnel for £25,000?" I increased the price because I felt if you can sell for 10k you can sell for 25k+. On a whiteboard he had an archway drawn out with A on the left and B on the right. A was where they were now - a funnel builder that can't sell a marketing funnel for £5000 yet alone £25,000. B was where they could close a customer for £25,000+ confidently. A was the start and B was the end.

In very simple terms, he asked me "what's the first step? What's the second step?" and so on. Before I knew it, I had the letter A written six times on my notepad. It was like a brilliant shining light on the page. The process that I struggled to find or put into words was in front of me the whole time. It was my 6A framework for my own business. Whenever we put together a new campaign to sell a new service or start a new funnel offer, we followed this framework.
- Audience
- Amount
- Assets
- Authority
- Attention
- Action

This 6A framework is what I'm going to teach you in this book. We'll start with Audience and work through to Action. Helping you attract and close leads, increase your prices and sell a marketing funnel for five figures. It's the internal framework that I used for years to explain why we did or didn't make any sales and made sure that I had everything I needed before I went out to market. It's done me very well over the years and I believe it can fix your funnel business.

I've got a free custom report available at sellyourservice.co.uk/focus which can tell you your 6A Score. It'll rank where you are now for every one of the 6A's and tell you where to focus next. It's totally free and you can find it at sellyourservice.co.uk/focus. I'm very excited to share this with you. It's been my favourite book to write to date, and I can't wait to hear what amazing progress you're going to make.

Email me michael@sellyourservice.co.uk with any questions.

Have courage, commit, take action.

Mike Killen

AUDIENCE

Without question, the absolute first thing that funnel builders (and all businesses for that matter) must define first, is their audience. The group of people that will listen to you, follow your advice and buy from you.

In this chapter you're going to learn how to define and create your audience, combine it with what you're great at and give your business a unique angle that makes it harder for competitors to encroach on you. We call this combination a niche.

An industry is not a niche

When we talk about choosing a niche for our marketing funnel business, the first place most people go to is an industry. I want to show you how to create a niche for your business that positions you as the #1 player in your market, without relying on an industry to define that niche.

Marketing funnel agencies and funnel builders who have invented a niche can demand higher fees, choose the projects they work on and attract clients easier. One of the common mistakes I see a lot of funnel builders make is thinking that they need to have the best product or service in order to increase their price. Or maybe they need more experience, or time on the market. The truth is that from today onwards, the only marketing funnel businesses that are profitable will be the ones who define and create a niche that no one else wants to serve.

When you define a niche, it's almost impossible to negotiate against you with price or terms of delivery. If you're sick of clients telling you what you should do, you need to invent a niche that you dominate. When you create a niche, you're instantly the #1 player in that market. If you need heart surgery and you talk to the world's #1 heart surgeon regarding your particular condition and procedure, you don't ask them for a discount. You also don't tell them what you think the best course of action is. You listen to them, let them do their job and you're happy with the results. When it comes to being #1 in a market, you don't care whether your surgeon is a good driver or what kind of music they listen to. They're so clearly the perfect, or even the *only* option that you just want them to focus on you and your situation. That's the benefit of being in a niche.

Creating a niche creates massive depth in your market. It's easier to create content that attracts new leads and visitors to your website. You're also more quickly recognised as an expert because you're focusing on one subject. Marketing funnel builders have a wide range of expertise, but when you focus on a niche, and you do nothing but talk about that niche, you become known for that niche.

If you want to be known as the garage that restores 1960's red Ferraris to showroom condition, then you better be sure to *just* talk about restoring 1960's red Ferraris to showroom condition. Don't mix the message with other brands of cars or other colours. Stick to what you want to be known for. Being known as a 'brand' is crafted over years of repeated, consistent messaging and delivering on expectations over and over. Choosing a niche and repeatedly sticking to the same message over and over in multiple formats and media is the best way to become known as a brand from something.

What is Richard Dawkins known for? It's atheism. Why? It's because all he does is talk about atheism. Yes, his books cover more and his lectures cover biology and philosophy and other subjects but he is predominantly known for atheism because that's the message he sticks to over and over and over.

When we go after a niche, the first place our mind races to is an industry. We think accountants, lawyers, architects, builders, restaurants, manufacturing, taxis, travel, tourism and catering. We immediately define the potential niches as segments defined by industries. Going after an industry will kill your marketing funnel business.

Not all businesses within an industry have similar characteristics

The biggest flaw with going after an industry is that there are few defining characteristics between multiple companies within one industry. Let's take manufacturing for example. There is a small welding equipment manufacturing business near my home in Devon, England. They probably employ a few hundred people across their group. By government standards they are considered a medium size business. However there are almost no similarities between their manufacturing business and 3M, one of the largest manufacturing companies on the planet.

Their internal business processes, their business structure, payments, staff hierarchy, tax requirements and other characteristics within their business would be too different to target. Their marketing and funnel needs would be too different for you to find a common delivery process. It even goes beyond what their marketing needs are or even what the strategy for their need is. Their goals are totally different. A business at £5 million in revenue has a totally different goal from a £31 billion revenue company.

If you want to work within an industry, you need to find more characteristics that define and connect your ideal market. We'll talk about that later in this chapter.

Industries die and grow

Industries have a nasty habit of following economic trends. One minute the housing market is booming and the next, your real estate agent is working part time at a bar. At the start of the year, the financial tech industry could be experiencing record growth, only to see dozens or hundreds of companies die before the year is out. It happens a lot and it won't stop happening. The way you protect yourself from these industry trends is to find characteristics across multiple businesses, outside of what their industry is.

How many businesses close sales deals on the phone? How many companies deliver their work to customers over a 12 month period and charge per month? How many businesses create a product with a 10 year guarantee? These are all characteristics that you can target and help; they are external to an industry.

However, wouldn't it make sense to work in an industry that's growing? Of course it would, and your marketing funnel product could easily target a growing industry. So, if you only sell to high end audio equipment manufacturers (as it's growing it looks great) when the industry takes a turn (and they do - they all do), you're left with a brand which is known for something that could be harder to transition into other areas. If instead, you say that you work with businesses that improve the audio experience of commuters, then you can work with high end audio engineering companies, app developers, transport businesses, clothing, materials manufacturing and more.

Most industries don't have a niche themselves

One of the most difficult aspects of targeting an industry is that most businesses within that industry don't have a niche themselves. This becomes a problem when you're looking to help that particular business grow. Typically, businesses that define themselves as a player in the X industry are relying on customers knowing what they want to buy. Most businesses in the welding manufacturing industry for example, won't have a niche. This is because they expect customers and prospects to know when they need a welding solution and to search out their options by themselves. Trouble is: NO industry is safe from genuine disruption from a new player in a market that dominates a category and captures the minds of an audience.

Food delivery. Legal. Transport. Holiday booking. Accountants. Publishing. Accommodation. Real Estate. Banking. Video publishing. Video games. Alcohol. These are some of the biggest industries in the world and every single one of them has been irrevocably changed forever by the introduction of a new player who themselves understood the power of defining a niche.

High Street Banking, despite rising and collapsing multiple times, is now under massive threat from mobile app banking which provides better rates, easier access to money and 24 hour support. Every other high street bank competed against each other with laughably low interest rates and occasionally lending money. They tried to define themselves within a market and separate themselves from their competition with celebrity spokespeople, TV adverts and as I mentioned, awful interest rates.

What's killing them now is that some banks are promising 24 hour support, financial management tools and an app. It took a few months to completely change the landscape of a 400 year old institution. What separated Barclays from HSBC from Chase from BOA? Nothing. However, when another business comes along and clearly states:

"Clever budgeting. Easy travel. Interest on your savings. And human help, whenever you need it."

Monzo.

I don't even care if it's a bank. It's speaking to my needs, rather than defining itself as another offering in an industry. It's not a high street bank; it's not even a bank; it's offering help with my finances. If you go after an industry, you'll quickly find that someone is going to flip it on its head and you won't have anything to offer the growing segment of that industry.

Most industries have a leader already

Industries that immediately come to mind are usually the same ones for most people, like we've mentioned above. Food, logistics, travel, legal, accountants, banks, charities, publishing, media. These large industries usually have a market leader in the field of 'Marketing' already. Some of these industries are so well served that 'Marketing for logistics' is almost its own industry. I don't believe that it's impossible to displace the #1 position for a marketing service leader within an industry, but it does take a LOT of money and time. Usually because large corporate businesses loathe risk and if they've been using Deloitte or IBM for years (even decades) they're unlikely to change.

On the other hand, I'd argue that going head to head with a bigger industry leading marketing business isn't as tough as it might seem. It's closer to the story of David and Goliath than you might realise. If David went head to head against Goliath on raw strength, he'd have been destroyed. But David didn't go head to head on strength, he used his speed (and deception). David brought new rules to the game and forced the rules of engagement to change. Using speed and his tools, he knocked Goliath down.

Rather than competing feature to feature with the bigger industry leaders, you're more likely to win business when you create new rules to play by. Some people call this 'category creation'. David wasn't interested in being the world's #2 best fighter against Goliath because #2 means you're dead. But if you asked "Who's the #1 slingshot expert in the world right now?" you'd think of Dave.

You've got the tools and agility that older and larger businesses don't have. You've got advantages that look like weaknesses. Even if you're a 350-person organisation, you're new to the market and that's a massive advantage if you use it well. What too many businesses do (and I'll assume that you're not a 350-person marketing organisation) is use the same tactics and strategies that larger businesses use to attract clients. If you're going after an industry, you're going to need to change how they engage with you. And that means removing the industry from your niche.

David didn't use strength which was the industry. He used tools and speed. Instead of working in the logistics division and going against big marketing companies using logistics, you could offer businesses that have a fleet of over 500 vehicles a way to increase their 'on the road' time. We'll talk more about wording your niche and choosing one later but if you can remove industry wording from your niche, you'll find a niche much faster.

Most well-known industries aren't good targets anyway because of their structure

At this point I'm sure you're already convinced that targeting a particular industry isn't worth your time. But in case you're not, I want you to think about the structure of a large business in a well known industry. If it's an industry that's commonly known, chances are it's a huge behemoth of corporations and conglomerates. If you've ever worked with one of those businesses, you know how awful they are to work for. I'm sure there are exceptions, but on the whole, they're pretty difficult to work for.

They don't even have to be a big business, they could be smaller businesses with only a few hundred employees. And I'm not saying you shouldn't target them. But beware of payment terms, long drawn out contracts and legal negotiations and never dealing with just one decision maker. When your marketing business just targets an industry, you're more likely to be treated as a commodity. You need to invent a niche to combat typical bad business practices. You're the leading expert in '500 vehicle fleet road time' or 'recurring revenue conversion for businesses that use crowd sourced staff'. Inventing a niche let's you move away from being treated like everyone else because you're *not* like everyone else.

Anything not everything

I don't doubt that every business in the world would benefit from working with you. Given the right amount of time and money, I'm sure you could help absolutely anyone. However, you can't help everyone.

"You can do anything – but not everything."

David Allen

Focusing is a complex and never ending pursuit. For example, to focus on the task at hand right now such as reading this book, all the way to focusing on a single niche. When it comes to working on a niche for your marketing business, you will always be tempted to try other niches. That's your scarcity reflexes kicking in. I believe people pick any industry niche or another broad definition because they want to hoard as much of the potential market as possible. It's like trying to hug a mountain. Your arms might be stretched as much as possible, but no one else has noticed. You're only going to make things harder for yourself. Instead, let's get massive penetration within a market and become the absolute undisputed leader of that niche. Rather than trying to help everyone.

We'll talk a bit later about the customer/product matrix and its impact on marketing ROI. However for your business, going after multiple types of customers with multiple types of products is a very, very expensive way to run a business. Another reason I believe people trick themselves into thinking their definition is a 'niche', when really it's massively broad (like the examples below) is because it's easy to stay busy but not really doing anything productive. When you've got a massive market, you can spend years researching and networking and talking to people. If I give you a hyper-specific niche and that's what you've got to go after, it's harder to ignore the fact that now you've got to approach and sell to that market. People use a broad or undefined niche as a way to create busy work for themselves. Picking a broad niche is a method of procrastination.

Don't worry about the market being too small

I want to give a few examples of some poor niche choices but before that, I want to answer the little voice in your head asking "But what if I choose a niche that's too small?" It's a valid question and to be honest, you're unlikely to fall into that trap if you follow my niche rules later on. Yes, if you've decided to *just* focus on 'email list growth for bakeries in Wrexham' you're unlikely to find hundreds of potential customers.

Years ago it made sense to be a generalist. To be a hardware store that sold multiple products to multiple types of customers made sense. You were limited to the geographic distance that people were willing to travel. If you just sold hammers, no matter how good those hammers were, people wouldn't travel more than 10-20 miles to buy from you. And how often do you buy a hammer? Or if you just sold to people who owned a 3 storey Victorian townhouse, then you're limited to how many of those customers are within a certain radius.

But now, with the internet, we can find hyper-specific micro markets that can sustain our business and grow us to six and seven figure revenues. I want to point out that we're looking for a hyper-specific micro *market*. Market is the key term here. NOT product. If someone sets up an online shop that just sold hammers, they're defining their business by the product they sell. Instead, we're going to define our business by the markets we serve. E.g. the types of people who *buy* those products. An online hammer shop could become 'home tools for people who'd rather die than hire a handyman'.

If you found a market of 1000 people that love you enough to give you £1000 a year, that's a £1 million business. If you found a market of 100 people that love you enough to give you £10,000, that's a £1 million business. We want specificity. We want hyper targeted and micro. Yes, Grant Cardone is probably the world's #1 sales trainer in the world (or Belfort, who cares?) at the moment. But Mike Killen is THE #1 sales trainer for funnel builders in the world.

Small business isn't a niche

If you're convinced that you need to select a hyper-specific micro niche, I want to clear off a few examples that aren't niches. If you read this book and ever EVER tell anyone that you work with 'small businesses', I'll personally consider this book a failure. *Small business* is not a niche. Small businesses account for a massive portion of all markets. It's way too massive to be considered a niche. It's like saying your target customer is a female.

Service industry isn't a niche

"Well, if Mike doesn't like small business, what about going after the service industry that's defined?" This is having your cake and eating it. Saying you're targeting the service industry is when you like the idea of targeting a niche but your scarcity reflexes have told you to stay broad. It's when you don't commit to the idea. Saying your niche is the service industry is like signing up to a gym and never going. You will never ever, ever see results and you'll never be known for anything. Here are some of the industries within 'the service industry'.

- Information Technology
- Hospitality
- Travel
- Transportation
- Media
- Entertainment
- Sports
- Healthcare
- Wellness
- Finance
- Insurance
- Professional Services
- Consulting & Staffing
- Design
- Marketing & Sales
- Energy
- Management
- Information
- Markets
- Retail
- Ecommerce
- Culture
- Education
- Asset Rentals
- Product as a Service[1]

Service industry doesn't seem as well defined now does it?

'Start Ups' isn't a niche

Start Ups are a great example of an industry that love people helping them and make an easy sale but a lousy customer. One of the biggest traps you'll

---

[1] Taken from https://simplicable.com/new/service-industry

fall into is thinking that just because people are always looking for help does not mean you've found a customer. Charities, NGOs and freelancers all fall into this category. The reason I don't think you should target start Ups, is two fold:

Usually, they don't have customers. They might have funding, they might have investors and money in the bank but they don't have *customers*. Finding new customers for a new product is a very expensive and long process. They'll expect you to find them a market, sell products, attract customers and create an offer when they themselves aren't sure of who they're going after. And when it fails, they'll blame you.

They will ask for a discount or money off because they're a 'Start Up'. They'll say they're strapped for cash or just starting out. Great, let them start out. You're going to work with customers who can pay you.

Defining a niche attracts other niches

Finally, before we get into the niche definition process, there is a marketing concept called 'marketing continuum'. Marketing continuum is when you take a grid and plot your 'Target Market Options' along the top and 'Problems' on the side. We could focus on hundreds of different target markets and hundreds of different problems. 'New Leads' is a problem. 'Sales Conversions' is a problem. 'Cost Per Click' is a problem. 'Coaching Products' is a target market. 'Scalable SaaS Products' are a target market. 'Businesses With 1500 YouTube Subscribers' are a target market.

Problems/ Targets	Coaching products	YouTube creators	Saas businesses	Over 10000 email leads
New leads				
High ticket sales				
Low traffic levels				
Zero strategy				
Stressed				

Figure 1: Marketing Continuum Table

When we cross-check each problem/target market, we're given an option to create a product or content or an offer to that niche. What tends to happen is people will *spread* their products, offers and content across the grid. They'll put a little in each area, fooling themselves into calling it 'market diversification' or 'product suite' when really, it doesn't build momentum or density in any one area.

However, if you chose one square by combining one problem with one target market, for example, email list growth for 'Businesses With 1500 YouTube Subscribers' and you put all your efforts into that one area, you'll build **density**. It'll become like a black hole or neutron star. It'll become dense with products and offers and content. And what do black holes do? They pull in planets and matter and even light past a certain point. They suck in everything. And that's what happens with a well defined niche.

When you commit to a niche and create products, offers and content within one area, you will begin to attract other niches. The fastest way to work in other areas is to commit heavily to one. All of a sudden, our niche of email list growth for 'Businesses With 1500 YouTube Subscribers' will have people asking "Can you do the same for me?" It'll be up to you if you work with them or not. But if you're afraid of creating too small a niche, don't. You will affect the marketing continuum with your hyper focused attention to one niche. It'll draw in opportunities from other areas.

Choose a part of the process

We're going to create a niche out of thin air. And the biggest problem is our traditional thinking around what a niche is. Your niche for your marketing funnel business isn't just something you go after and sell products to. It's what *you* become. YOU need to become your niche. It sounds unintuitive and can be confusing to both create what you become and create what you go after, but after we've done this exercise you'll see how you both become and attract the niche you create.

A niche is a problem you solve or a result you get for a group of people with certain characteristics that no one else wants to serve. It could be both a problem you solve and a result you get, but there needs to be the critical component of a characteristic within a group of people that no one else wants to serve.

- Problem you solve
- Result you get
- Specific group of people
- Specific characteristics
- No one else wants to serve

This is where we hit our first major roadblock. We often mistake a niche as something that either already exists and is undiscovered, or something that someone else is already serving and we can go after that niche too. In truth, a true niche is something that *you* carve into the market. It's something that hasn't existed before you've defined it. However, when people see it they'll wonder why someone isn't already serving that niche.

For example, many people believe a niche is something that reveals itself to you, bathed in light, a holy sign from above as you stumble across it like the great city of El Dorado. It's as if we think there will be an undiscovered tribe of people with wads of cash in their pockets, just waiting for someone to sell them products. And when a business dominates a niche and serves a particular audience, their business explodes on the marketplace and it's because they discovered this profitable niche before anyone else. We mistakenly believe that we have to be the first to discover and claim a niche, like the Conquistadors colonising South America.

One example of a business that discovered and dominated a niche would be Harrys' Razors. Harry's Razors is a razor blade and shaving subscription service that provides razor blades, a handle, foam, moisturiser and other shaving gear. You can trial their set and service before doing a flexible, easy to understand razor blade subscription.

"But Mike, didn't Dollar Shave Club do this first?" Yep, they absolutely did. DSC was started in 2011 and started the idea of subscribing to a razor blade service that provided good quality blades at a fraction of the price. The beautiful part about Harry's is that they came later to a market and served an audience that DSC didn't want to - the UK and Europe. DSC could have entered the UK/EU market but they didn't. They do now of course, and since being bought by Unilever for £1 billion, DSC has spurned dozens of imitators. Harry's on the other hand did go into the UK and has been sold to Edgewell/Wilkinson Sword for £1.4 billion.

When we think 'subscription product for men's shaving to save time and money', we think that's an obvious niche. We think that of course you'd be successful in that niche because who *wouldn't* want to buy that? The problem is that no one else thought of it. The larger corporations like Unilever and Edgewell couldn't create something like that because they didn't want to see what niches were out there. The problem is that we don't discover niches, we create them.

Creating a niche is far slower and you don't get any feedback. There weren't groups of men sat around wondering "If only I could save money and have my razor blades sent to my door." It wasn't even an option. But as soon as someone asked them if they wanted it, it sounded like an obvious idea. Many large corporate businesses fail to understand that people aren't creative and inventive. Henry Ford said that if he listened to his customers, they'd ask him for a faster horse. Focus groups and customer brainstorming sessions don't work. Customer's can't think of more intuitive or better solutions because they don't even know what's possible. That's not having a go at anyone, I'm the same of course. If someone asked me what I could do to make my shaving experience better, I would have said cheaper blades. But when a solution like Harry's is put in front of me I ask myself "Why didn't someone think of this before?"

Our niche needs to be the same. It's created, not discovered. It's *invented*, rather than stumbled upon by chance. And we're going to create that niche right now. If you want to download the first niche worksheet for free, head to sellyourservice.co.uk/fivefigurefunnels. Or grab a piece of paper and draw a line down the centre of the page. Write 'Start' at the top and 'End at the bottom.

This line is a timeline of every marketing funnel project that you've worked on. I want you to imagine a project with unlimited time and unlimited budget. A perfect client who will use all and every part of the funnel process for their business. Write out each stage of the marketing funnel process that you could deliver to a customer. Think about all the individual marketing funnel activities, campaigns, automations and features that a business would use and write them down.

It might help to start at the end. Thinking about sales pages and upsells and sales campaigns. Then work backwards to the start where we have activities like paid cold traffic, email subscribers and warm traffic remarketing. On the left hand side of the timeline, I want you to write the activities and actions that you LIKE to do. Things you're happy to create for customers and work on. For example, I like creating email campaigns and sales pages. List as many as you can. Things that you like or even love to do as work for your customers. Maybe it's stuff you just get, something that you like to do for customers and they say you're "passionate" about. That's everything you list on the left hand side.

On the right hand side, list off what you're good at. Activities and campaigns that you're capable of delivering to customers. You don't have to like them or love them, but I want you to write out every activity that, if push came to shove, you *could* deliver to customers. Of course you'd rather do stuff that you love. You can of course write things down that you're good at AND you love to do, that's fine. But on the right hand side of the timeline, write out everything you're good at. A good indicator of this is the question "Would someone pay me for this?"

I've got an example of my list below. Remember, we've created a timeline of activities starting with topics such as cold traffic from SEO and warm remarketing, right down to sales campaigns. What this exercise does is help us focus on one part of the marketing funnel process. A common misconception is that if we're a funnel business or that we build marketing funnels, we must build *every* part of the marketing funnel and that's not true. Let me explain why.

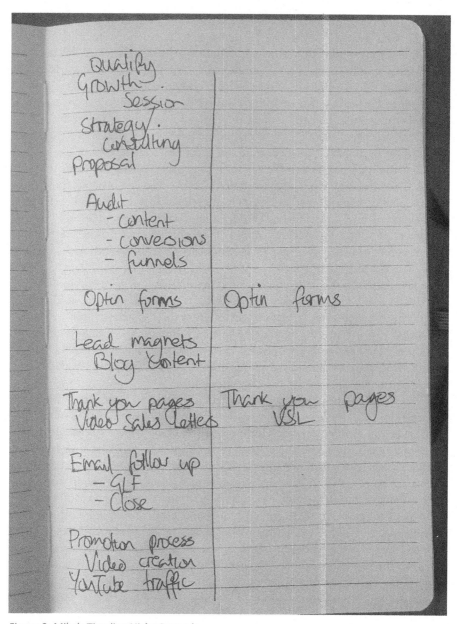

Figure 2: Mike's Timeline Niche Example

Our job is to focus on a result for customers. We want to help our customers get a certain result and I've talked before in my book From Single To Scale, about how 'results ≠ delivery'. What this means is that the results we get for customers are not exclusive to the way we deliver those results. While we start by looking at a particular activity, such as email marketing, we'll dig deeper into the results and benefits of that activity, as well as who it's most suitable for. For example, email marketing really works with generating sales from leads and sales from current customers, but not so well for generating cold traffic or for new subscriber attraction. What we can now say is that we help businesses with their sales for products. The result is that we increase sales. The delivery at the moment might be email marketing and yes, email is unlikely to go away for a long time. However, at one point, people thought that cold traffic ads to landing pages was the best way to grow a list. Now we know we can't do that. So, if we focused on cold traffic ads for building lists the old way and we exclusively said that we offer the 'delivery' of cold traffic ads to landing pages, we're outdated as soon as the delivery method becomes unviable. If instead we focused on telling people that we help businesses build their email list, we're always valuable, even if the delivery method changes.

We start with the delivery method because many of these techniques and activities won't be outdated any time soon. However, we're going to discover a group of people that we want to serve rather than an activity that we enjoy. It's easier to invent a niche starting from an activity rather than a group of people. Take link building for SEO a few years back. That was the #1 way to rank your website - linking as many sites as possible to yours, both linking from external websites and to other sites.

Nowadays however, while high quality link building is absolutely a critical part of an SEO strategy, long term authenticity, lots of regular content and unique content tends to play a larger role in ranking pages on Google. If we defined our business by the activity of link building, we'd have to redefine what it is we offer to the market as soon as link building becomes obsolete. Instead, we're going to discover a result and subsequently a group of people that benefit from that result, to create a niche and dominate a market.

Your timeline should have a list of things you enjoy doing and a list of things you're good at or that people will pay you for. Our job is to focus on one element of the marketing funnel process and create a niche around that part of the process. Look for one activity that overlaps both 'love to do' and 'good at'. This is your ideal activity. Something that you enjoy doing and you get paid for because you're good at it. It might be you have a few that overlap and that's absolutely fine.

Ideally, we're looking for one activity to start with and we can always expand out later. For the time being, just select one. If you have two or more activities that are similar to each other, you can group them together but my advice is to focus on one hyper-specific activity. Finally, occasionally we see overlaps or intersections between activities. Later, we're going to look at activities for ourselves like public speaking, course creation and consulting.

Don't worry for the time being how you deliver results to your customer, just focus on one activity that you're going to work from.

Who benefits from your focus?

When you've selected a part of the process that you're going to work on, we now need to start creating an offer that we'll take to a market. Most businesses will only go so far as to determine their deliverables, rather than delve deeper into their niche. When we go to market, we want to tell people <u>who</u> we work with and how they benefit, not just what we do.

There are degrees of effectiveness with a niche. Starting at the bottom, the least effective definition of a niche is telling people what you do in a broad sense. This is typically when you tell people that you run a marketing business or a marketing funnel agency. The next level, which while being slightly more effective, still leaves a lot to be desired, is to focus on one aspect as we've done above. For example, "I focus on email marketing for small businesses". This may be your sweet spot of what you do but it isn't appealing to an audience or customer. It's also much harder to generate referrals. Unless someone already understands the power of your chosen area, they're unlikely to know how it benefits them. The only thing that human beings are interested in, is what's in it for them?

Figure 3: Niche Effectiveness Pyramid

"WIIFM? Or What's In It For Me? Is the most
played radio station in the world."

Zig Ziglar

When you talk to people your niche needs to be something that tells people one of two things: Either that it will be worth their time and energy to talk to you, or that they shouldn't talk to you. When we talk to people and tell them what we do, even if we've specified a certain area, their brain is asking "How does this benefit me?" and unless you can either tell them it will, they'll assume that it won't. When we have a broad niche or mission we think we're playing it safe and that less people will be turned off. Instead, because it's unfocused, it *does* turn people off and they're less engaged. It's a funny world.

We need to add further characteristics and qualifiers to our sweet spot/chosen process in order to better define our niche. These characteristics include but are not limited to:

- Product types
- Conversion we can improve
- Process, activity or campaign
- Type of business
- Problem they're facing
- What the business wants
- Types of customer's customer
- Their characteristics
- Their business level/maturity
- The results they get for customers

When we combine and stack these traits we create a compelling and distinct niche. Of the three examples below which sounds more appealing to work with? Who sounds like they know what they're doing?

1. We are a digital marketing company
2. We do email marketing for small businesses
3. We work with businesses about to publish their second book who are turning that into an online course and we help them convert book sales into recurring revenue course customers.

Of those examples, which sounds easier to create content for? Which one sounds easier to find a market for, or a large audience? Who do you think has a higher fee for a standardised process? Who sounds more like an expert?

Number 3 has a defined niche. And the litmus test is to ask "Who do you work with?" Number 3 can answer that when Numbers 1 and 2 can't. When people ask "What do you do?" they're really asking "Who do you work with?" and that's what we need to be able to answer. As we've covered above, small business and local business is not a niche. A niche is a problem solved or result achieved for a group of people with certain characteristics that no one else wants to help.

When we have our sweet spot, in our example case Email Marketing, we need to then find a group of people or *things* that benefit from that process. Firstly, we'll cover off what we mean by those traits above and give a few examples. Then, we'll go through the process of discovering who benefits the most from working with you and therefore, who is our niche.

Product types

There are so many product types that it's almost overwhelming to think about them. Product types refers to the different methods of delivering results and services to customers and the different price points and levels of engagement that customers will experience. For example, a book is a product type from a well known world class speaker. But working with customers one-on-one is another product type. Certain types of products suit certain processes better and you might find that you enjoy one product over another. Products can be free, like webinars and blog posts or they can cost millions of dollars. This list below isn't exhaustive but it's a good start.

- Splinter products
- Lead magnets
- Webinars
- Core physical product offers
- Subscription products
- Customer win backs
- Refunds
- Up-sells/Cross-sells
- Digital downloads
- Physical products
- High ticket items
- Workbooks and programs
- Live events
- Marketplaces
- Auction sites
- Job boards

Conversion we can improve

Conversions relate to each stage of the marketing funnel and the specific transition between that stage. For example, this book helps with sales conversions, specifically core product sales (assuming your £25,000 marketing funnel is a core offer). Getting new people to read a blog post is a traffic conversion, from 'never heard of them' to 'first time reader'. Typically this is called cold traffic. Your process will suit and be beneficial to only a few conversions. It might even only work with one or you might find that you love increasing one particular type of conversion:

- Attracting cold/warm traffic
- Social followers/subscribers
- Email list subscribers
- First time sales
- Repeat sales
- Refunds
- Email engagement/social engagement
- Leads/prospects
- Low ticket sales
- High ticket sales
- Upsells/X-sells
- Affiliate sales

Process, activity or campaign

Your customers have a lot of different campaigns and activities they're working on themselves. There are processes that they need to get done each day, week or month - everything from creating advertising campaigns to creating blog content. The number of businesses who write proposals or update their own website is massive. If there is a time-consuming activity that they could get someone else to take care of, they'll do it.

- Creating social content
- Writing blog posts
- Customer support
- Customer onboarding
- Collecting testimonials
- Writing proposals
- Running webinars
- Creating adverts
- Selling to customers
- Account management

Type of business

There are many more businesses than just small, medium and big. Rather than size I prefer to think about the deliverable or type of work that businesses 'do'. Rather than their industry, it's a question of what they give to their customers. What features does that business hand to their customer? Do they sell them physical products that require maintenance? Do they deliver education to customers? Do they give customers books or apps or clothing? What I love about these questions is that it transcends industry. The car, audio, medical, mining and video game industry all have products that fit those questions above but not all businesses deliver the same features within an industry.

- SaaS businesses
- Online courses
- Coaching
- Physical exercise
- Writers and authors
- Manufacturing
- Design and branding
- Coding and development
- Communities
- Medical and veterinary
- Application and software
- Content publishing
- PLR or public label rights
- White-label
- Outsourcing

Problem they're facing

Most businesses tend to face similar groups of problems. While the specifics might vary from business to business, in general they tend to be trying to solve a particular set of problems that are universal. One of the reasons I love looking at the problem a business faces and using that within our niche, is because it transcends business size and industry and lets us focus on something that the business recognises. For example, the problem of 'too many refunds' might be shared by massive telco corporations or smaller online course businesses.

- Not enough traffic
- Not enough walk-ins
- Low client retention

- Not enough time
- Not enough steady cash flow
- Stuck in feast/famine
- Low number of leads/enquiries
- Low project budget size
- Low lead quality
- Struggle with technical help
- Not enough recurring revenue/stability

Note that problems often start with 'low' or 'not enough'. Problems and needs can sometimes be mixed up and confused. For example, a business might feel that their biggest problem is that they don't have enough high quality leads. They might also feel that they *need* high quality leads, but the solution to 'not enough leads' is not 'get more leads'. For your niche and ideas I want you to focus on something your customers are suffering from or they don't have enough of. Which problem is easiest to solve, using your chosen part of the process?

What the business wants

Wants and needs are two very different things. Sometimes they're the same thing, but as a rule you can't sell someone something they need unless they want it. People only buy what they want, even if it's not the right thing. As funnel businesses, you know that your customers need a content and traffic strategy combined with a strong sales automation process, but your customers *want* increased cash flow and sales. We can go one further, and if we're getting to know our customers, it might be that what they truly want is a deeper desire that they're not expressing. Almost all businesses want sales, leads, traffic and more time. But more often than not we're selling to the business owner or a decision maker. What *they* want is to sell the business and retire or to grow the business and attract investors. If you can appeal to what a business decision maker really wants, you'll find attracting interested leads and standing out in a market much easier.

- Grow to become a global news source
- Open in multiple locations
- Start a franchising
- Become a slowpreneur/author/'status'
- Help more people without sacrificing their own life
- More freedom
- No worry about online course delivery and management
- A business that supports their life, but doesn't consume it
- Grow an email list

- Increase sales
- Move leads to sales
- Grow and scale their business
- Become visible in a crowded market
- Lead generation, enquiries
- Generate leads, contact info
- Grow an Email List to Market to for others
- More leads and sales
- Increase revenue
- Increase profit

I'd advise you to really think about a want or desire that affects the decision maker's emotions, daily life and status. Too many marketing businesses tell the market that they help increase traffic or leads or sales. It's a weak position to be in because EVERY marketing business is designed to increase one of those metrics. However, when you define your niche through the inner desires, goals and dreams of the people you'll be working with, that's a very different offer. Which desire or want is more suitable for your chosen sweet spot?

Types of client's customer

Our clients have customers and when we can define our market by the type of customer that our clients want to attract, we can easily define a corner of the market that other marketing businesses don't want to touch. All businesses have a mixture of customer types, from customers who subscribe to a recurring payment product, to customers who have bought one product and never returned. As a marketing agency we can define our niche as specialists who help X businesses attract more high-ticket customers or who allow businesses to generate an extra 50% in sales from unhappy customers. Think about your chosen part of the process and ask "Which type of customer would be more likely to engage or buy if I used my sweet spot?"

- New customers
- Long time customers
- Customers who have left
- Un-engaged customers (people who have bought but never consumed)
- Subscription customers
- High ticket customers
- White-whales (people who buy EVERYTHING you put out)
- Promoters and evangelists (super fans who love what you do)
- Loyal customers

- Unhappy and disgruntled customers
- Personal contact services (think personal trainers)
- Off the shelf/cookie cutter products

Their characteristics/what they need to have

Businesses in an industry might have almost no shared characteristics other than their industry label which is one of the reasons I don't think industry is a good place to define your niche. However, there might be characteristics within a business that are suitable for you to work in and that your chosen sweet spot can add massive value to. For example, maybe if your chosen sweet spot is split testing sales pages to increase conversions. That part of the funnel process is way more beneficial to someone who is already generating sales. If you work with a customer who has low or no sales, it'll take a long time to see if your split testing really adds anything. Another way of phrasing this question is asking yourself "If I didn't get paid until after the customer got results, what would they need to have in order for me to work with them?"

Imagine not getting paid until after your client got results. Your chosen sweet spot is split testing. What would they need to have already in order for you to do your work and get them great results as fast as possible? I learnt this from Frank Kern. It might be that there are a few different characteristics you need and that's great! We'll shorten the terminology for the characteristics or even come up with a 'tribe name' for them (a name for a group of people with shared characteristics) later. But for now I want you to think about shared characteristics that suit your process and would be recognised by potential customers. Remember, it's not about attracting everyone, it's about attracting the right people. Saying "We help businesses with over 1000 visits per sales page per day increase conversions in 30 days" is a very specific and attractive niche.

- Have an email list of #
- Have revenue of over #
- Have # staff
- Have remote staff or all in one location
- At least # products
- Products of value of at least # or between #
- Sell in # countries
- Have or don't have a marketing department
- Are or are not listed on a stock market
- Traffic of over # a month/year
- Have both physical and virtual stores
- Are only available online/in store

Their business level/maturity

Another defining trait you might use in your niche is the ideal customer age, level or maturity. As a rule, I tend not to work with Start Ups. Their message is often too flexible and it's too difficult to get them to nail down and commit to a long term growth plan. Also, getting a start up to seven figures is a massive level of work, often combined with investor backing and not having any customers to start with. However, I do like working with businesses at the £1M turnover level and have been on the market for over 5 years. I find that they're still young and small enough to do some cool activities but established enough to stand by their message and market. There are different ways to measure age or level or maturity. Don't let that confuse you too much, just look at what feels natural. Don't over complicate it. What kind of business would benefit the most from your sweet spot? Do they call themselves disruptors or eco-friendly? Are they enterprise level or struggling against market commoditization?

- Category leaders
- Disruptive
- Unique
- Commoditized and don't want to be
- Entry level
- Start ups
- Enterprise level
- New
- Established
- Specific and focused
- Diverse
- Unknown in their market

The results they get for customers

Finally, let's look at possibly the most definitive and attractive trait for your niche - your customers' results. What kind of results do they get for *their* customers? This is where we can really start to separate ourselves from our competition and rise above our market. It also is a good place for you to look at the types of customers that you want to work with. For example, I'm not really bothered about entertainment and entertaining people. Gambling, video streaming and e-sports are massive markets but I just don't care enough about them to help businesses attract more attention in that market. However, I love helping businesses that help their customers generate wealth. I work with funnel builders and marketing businesses (like you!) that help *their* customers become wealthier. You might be really into health and fitness, so you like to help businesses who help *their* customers become fitter and healthier. You don't have to look at it like that. You could of course look at your sweet spot and see what kind of customer result would benefit the most, or what result could your process scale out?

At its core, there are five types of results that your customers are getting for their customers. Health, wealth, relationships, hobbies and status. Health is both mental and physical. Wealth is freedom through the use of money. Relationships is anything to do with other people. Hobbies are the things we spend money on to enjoy ourselves and status is what we are or become. All businesses predominantly fall into one of these five categories. What types of businesses do *you* want to work with? My customers help *their* customers with…

- Physical results
- Financial results
- Self help and improvement
- Market results
- Measurable results (email list, traffic)
- Clarity and consulting
- Content creation and publishing
- Safety and security
- Adrenaline
- Exposure and publicity
- Break records
- Customer acquisition
- Money management
- Dietary health improvement
- Competitive edge in the market
- Increase knowledge
- Create the status as a great and reliable vendor
- Home Improvement
- Clear view of their financial status and future
- Brand exposure
- Improved health, feel better, feel more accomplished, help the environment
- Quality of life improvement
- Making drastic external change
- Leadership
- Improved comfort in their home
- Bragging to family and friends

It's not easy and it might take a while to run through but I want you to select at least one trait from each category that your process will add the most value to. We might not stick to that trait or use it in our niche statement but it's valuable to challenge yourself and think about who really benefits the most from your process. That's your niche. That's how we start to rise above the market noise and compete in an increasingly commoditized market.

Niche Statement Builder

Once you have your list of traits it's time to build a niche statement that tells people who you work with. This will be your ideal target audience within your market. We've shown earlier how 'your niche' is not just the people you go after, but it's what you become. You carve your niche into a market and it will fit certain people. You are that carving, you're that weird ugly shape in a flat market that suits some people, just fine. In fact, they'll feel more comfortable fitting into the niche you've carved and will reward you because of that.

A niche is a problem solved or a result achieved for a specific group of people with certain characteristics that no one else wants to serve. We need to be comfortable turning down 99% of the market to attract 1% and we will become leaders to that 1%. Try not to think of the niche as the people you're attracting, but rather the tribe that you're all a part of. You're a leader within a tribe rather than discovering the tribe. You're attracting people to your way of life rather than finding a group of people who are already together and trying to lead them.

Let's break down the niche definition above: A problem solved or a result achieved for a specific group of people with certain characteristics that no one else wants to serve. We're going to pick either a problem and/or a result, a group of people and a characteristic. Don't worry too much if this feels awkward or clunky at the moment, it's bound to feel uncomfortable if you're doing this for the first time. Play around with the statement and don't think you need to have it all done in one go. Many niches take multiple drafts and re-working. It's more important to begin than to get it perfect.

A problem solved

What is the core problem that your niche solves? For example, the commoditization of their market or that they never have enough time to go to the gym.

- Conversion we can improve
- Process, activity or campaign
- Problem they're facing
- What the business wants
- Their characteristics
- Their business level/maturity

A result achieved

What result do people in your market want and what are you going to help them get? Again, it could be a wider result that their business is looking for or something that the owner or decision maker is struggling with. Both the problem or result could be something specific that only certain businesses are facing, thus becoming more specific about your niche.

- Conversion we can improve
- Process, activity or campaign
- What the business wants
- Their characteristics

For a specific group of people

Who is the group of people you're trying to attract? Are you looking to serve CEOs? Businesses? Outdoor businesses? Wealth businesses? You can look at the industry but also try to focus on other defining groups that are large enough to recognise and easy to learn more about.

- Product types
- Process, activity or campaign
- Type of business
- Types of customer's customer
- Their characteristics
- Their business level/maturity
- The results they get for customers

With certain characteristics

You can either stick to the two or three categories above or add in further qualifiers to your niche. Perhaps combine multiple niche traits to define the specific role you play within your niche. Yes, you might work with CEOs who are new to the role and want to increase sales, but you might also focus on businesses that want to increase sales with physical media products.

- Product types
- Process, activity or campaign
- Type of business
- What the business wants
- Types of customer's customer
- Their characteristics
- Their business level/maturity
- The results they get for customers

That no one else wants to serve

And the final part to the equation is being able to say that your competitors either won't or can't go after that niche. We want to create a niche statement that makes everyone else in your market rethink their position because when you come out with a specific niche and tell people that's who you work with, they'll either do one of two things:

1. They'll double down on staying broad and they'll be too afraid to go as niche as you. They might even tell you that you're crazy to go so specific.
2. They'll create a niche of their own and further separate themselves from you.

Either way we want our competition to say the opposite to what we're saying. If we say that we only work with CEOs of health and wellbeing businesses to increase sales of weighted media products, our competition won't want to go after the same niche because we've demonstrated already that we are experts at what we do and therefore we're #1. To go after us would be mad.

The final part of the equation is the statement itself. Our niche is telling people *who* we work with, not what we do. It's the dent we carve into the market and who we define our business as. The statement itself needs to tell people who it is we can help EXCEPT, we're not going to use the work help.

"We help" is so overused. Everyone helps. That's the point of running a business. Instead I want you to think of another verb to replace the word help.

- We empower
- We assist
- We energise
- We motivate
- We focus

When you're telling people who you work with you can absolutely say "We work with ..." but when we turn the statement into an emotional, almost illogical passage it becomes far more powerful.

We allow busy Mum's who run digital course businesses to finish work by 3pm so they can collect their kids from school.

We energise high performance relationship coaches to scale their income without working longer hours.

We focus the marketing efforts of crowd-sourcing businesses to allow CEOs to sell and retire.

You have to read your niche statement and think "Yes, this is exactly who I want to work with and what I want to do every single day." But what if you can't define a niche? It's a good question and certainly something that I struggled with. What I did and what I tell others now is to start focusing on one area, ideally a customer type or a desired long term result. When I first started Sell Your Service I talked about WordPress businesses, graphic designers, digital marketers and more. It was a mess. And what I did was repeatedly create content. Over and over I'd write blog posts, record videos, record podcasts, present webinars and eventually my niche revealed itself to me. It wasn't an epiphany moment. There was no holy choir and call from above; it just became apparent to me that the more I talked about sales training for funnel builders who wanted to sell a five figure funnel, the more traction I gained. Those were the topics I looked forward to writing about. Those were the videos I wanted to record. So, I just kept doing that.

The niche isn't profitable

Just before we wrap up this chapter I want to talk about why your niche won't be profitable and we've talked about this already. There is an idea that you'll discover a magical tribe of people with cash in their pockets, desperate to buy from you as if a niche is something that's waiting to be discovered. And as you've seen, you don't discover a niche, you create a niche. If we're being pedantic with the wording, yes, you could argue that you discover it through creating it. Nevertheless, the massive difference between truth and fiction is that the niche doesn't exist until you label it. And your niche will be just as challenging and hard work as any other niche. It's not the niche that's profitable, it's your dedication to that niche.

"You can't build a reputation on what you are going to do."

Henry Ford

Too often new funnel businesses want all the benefits of trust, reputation and experience without building it. You need to start carving steps. If you want to be recognised as someone who is responsible for a set of steps carved up to the top of a mountain, you've got to carve the steps into the side of a mountain until you reach the top. There is absolutely no shortcut. No elevator. Everyone has to take the stairs. If you want the benefit of reputation and trust, you've got to start building it.

It's a long journey and it takes time. At first it'll seem like a massive effort to do one thing over and over but eventually you'll produce a reputation for getting results and you'll be known for something. How do you get there? How do we carve those steps or build a reputation? If you wanted to be known as the guy or girl who will carve a step into the side of a mountain every day, what do you think you'd need to do? It's not complex. There's no secret. If you want to be known for X, you have to do X every day for 1000 days. That's the secret to building a reputation. If you want to be known for being the world's best refund reducer or splinter product sales expert – do that every day. You need to commit to doing *something* every day that proves you know what you're talking about. Blog posts, video, podcasts, interviews, social posts, emails, whatever it takes. Your job is building a reputation.

Over time you build a library of information, valuable content that helps your audience. You haven't quit on them. You've seen it through. If you're going to do anything in your business ask yourself "Would I do this every day for 1000 days?" That's the gate. You have to be willing to do something every day for 1000 days. Your reputation is only built when you commit for 1000 times. At first you'll be unnoticed but quickly, you'll build a reputation as someone who does 'the thing' and does it well.

When we first started our blog posts were unfocused and had no clear audience, but I did them every day for a year. I wrote a blog post every day on marketing funnels for a year. Looking back now they're not great, but they're there. Now, we have the reputation as the sales blog for funnel builders. Same with YouTube. It's small now, but it's growing. The reputation is built on the past 100 or 500 or 999 times. It's not built on a 1000 times in the future.

Imagine you're standing at the base of the mountain. At the top of the mountain is your niche. The widest part at the foot of the mountain is the wider market. It's undefined, easier to climb, but also doesn't offer the best views. You know that you need to get to the top of the mountain, but you're surrounded by other funnel builders. Other marketers, web designers, developers. They've all heard about the riches and the views from the top. That's where most people think they want to be.

So, you all start climbing. However, you're taking a different route. You are just going to start carving steps into the side of the mountain. At first, within minutes, you will be all by yourself. Some people will have started ascending faster than you. They'll try and sprint up and a few will fall down straight away. Another group will insist that their new bike or machine will get them there faster. A few will laugh at you and tell you that you're crazy for starting this far down. "Start further up and get a head start" they'll tell you. Others will tell you it's a waste of time. A small fraction of people will also start to carve steps into the side of the mountain. Some because they want to copy you, others because they believe they have what it takes to get them to the top.

Eventually, you begin to get into a rhythm and you're carving a few steps a day. No matter what the weather is like, what the terrain is like, you carve at least one step into the side of the mountain. Some days, people will overtake you, other days you'll be ahead and looking up; there doesn't seem to be an end in sight. You even get to know a few of your climbers. Very shortly, people start giving up. "I've heard there's an easier mountain over there. It's faster to climb, you don't have to carve as wide or deep steps because it's easier. I'm heading over there" you'll hear them say. You can't believe people are giving up so easily. Then, more people start giving up. The sprinters who ran off ahead of you at the start are now climbing back down. "I couldn't get to the top. It's too difficult. I'm going to start climbing that mountain over there. I've heard it's much easier to get to the top."

You'll also start to pass people who have settled on the side of the mountain. They'll try to convince you to stop, to rest with them. They'll give you every reason and excuse in the book "The view isn't that great. I only wanted to get halfway up anyway. If you try to get to the top you'll lose your friends." History is littered with unnamed people who never reached the top.

On some days you'll absolutely want to give up; your tools will break; competitors will smash up your previous efforts and steps; you'll be able to see people passing you on this mountain and others tempting you back down. You'll even be able to see other mountains with tiny dots of people climbing them. "How are they doing that so fast?!" you ask. It's demoralising and hard work. You look at your step count and it's barely 500 - you're not even halfway. This is the great filter. The dip or trough that stops most people reaching the top. It's what stops businesses from going past 5 years. It's what prevents great athletes from achieving gold.

You'll bargain with yourself and tell yourself that here is good enough or that maybe that other mountain, that other opportunity or niche is a faster result, that you should quit while you're ahead. Don't quit yet. Keep going. It doesn't keep getting worse.

Eventually, you find yourself nearing the top. It begins to level off and is less steep. You're better and faster than ever at creating these steps. The weather clears and you can see progress being made. You'll still have people calling you crazy telling you that you must have cheated or that "It's easy for you because you already had 900 steps under your belt", but eventually it's obvious that this is where you should be.

The profit and riches weren't in the mountain; they weren't in the niche; they were in the steps you carved into the side of the mountain. You'll even find old staircases where the owner just gave up; it's covered in weeds and is crumbling apart. They were so close you think as you begin to finalise your ascent and carve those final steps. The profit isn't in the niche, it's in your dedication to the niche.

Summary

- You must define a niche if you want to raise your prices and attract more customers
- A niche is not an industry, nor is it small businesses or service businesses
- Your niche is a result achieved or problem solved for a group of people with specific characteristics that no one else wants to serve
- A niche only becomes profitable when you commit to it and serve it

AMOUNT

The confusion around pricing is particularly upsetting to me, as it becomes so over-complicated and marred with emotion. Despite being the most logical and formulaic part of selling and running a business, people get pricing confused with their feelings around money. In this chapter, we're going to strip back the pricing process and create a pricing model that is profitable, scalable and most importantly, specific to your business.

Define your price first

If you want to start charging five figures for your marketing funnels, or for any service for that matter, you need to start with the price. As counter intuitive as that sounds, you need to define your price before you decide what you want to sell.

What most marketing agencies and business owners do is decide the price after they've decided what they want to sell and that's what kills businesses. Deciding what you want to sell first sounds like the sensible thing to do. It even sounds like the *only* way to create a product or service. Surely you have to define what you're delivering to the customer before you decide what you're going to charge?

Here's what tends to happen: You're a marketing funnel agency and a new lead emails you asking for more information about your services. They tell you what they want and you agree to meet them for coffee to talk through their requirements. During the meeting (which runs way longer than 45 minutes), you talk through their ideas and you have a rough understanding of what they want.

You might even ask them about the budget to which they respond "We really don't know. We were hoping you'd be able to tell us what we should spend?" If you've been reading my blog (sellyourservice.co.uk) or watching my YouTube channel (youtube.com/sellyourservice) you know that's not a good enough answer, therefore you wait for a proper number and they tell you £5000, or £10,000 or whatever it is. It might be much more (it might be much much less) or they might still refuse to give you a firm number.

You leave the meeting feeling excited about the prospect of a new customer and some money coming in. You put off the proposal (because they're hard work) but eventually you write a list of things the customer needs. Email capture, email automation, squeeze pages, sales pages etc. Looking at the list you then try to think of a number for the price. It can't be too high, because you don't want the customer to recoil in horror and tell you it's a ludicrous price. That might lose you the deal right? A cheap customer in the hand is better than two in the bush. You'd rather price a little lower because you want to keep them interested. Maybe they'll spend more with you later? Besides, you can't price too high anyway, you don't have the experience yet. You know of other experts and agencies with way more experience than you and they struggle to charge even £5000 for their services.

No, it's better to play it safe and charge what you think sounds like a reasonable sum. You've decided what you're going to deliver and sell first, and now you're thinking of the price. That's the way it's always been done. You then send off the proposal to the customer. Maybe they respond quickly with "Thanks Mike, we'll take a look over this and let you know." Maybe you won't hear back from them for a while. Whatever happens, you chase them with a few emails and you hear back from them.

"Thanks for the quote Mike. We've heard back from a few other suppliers and your price was more than they're quoting. My nephew says he can do it for around £400."

Or "Mike, this price is over what we were expecting. It seems very expensive."

Or "Hi Mike. Thanks so much for the quote. Really excited to move forward. However, we understood that you're a freelancer so we can't afford to pay you. We'd be willing to give you lots of exposure and experience but we're just not able to pay such a high fee!"

These are all real examples of replies I've had by the way. No matter what I priced the proposal at, I would hear "That's too expensive." over and over. This led me to believe that customers didn't have the money. No way would I be able to charge such high prices. The competition for higher prices must be insane.

You're left with two options. Either drop your price to work with the customer because you need the cash flow, or lose the client and lose the money. And when you do work with the customer, who's complained about the price, are they easy to work with? Are they heck. They're a nightmare! They take ages to pay you, they question every little decision you make. Why would they hire a marketing professional only to challenge all your advice?

The reason they're difficult to work with is the same reason they challenged the price. This is a lot of money *to them* and they don't want to lose it. They have a scarcity based mindset, based around loss. If they don't try to control every aspect of how the money is spent, they're more likely to lose it in their mind. When you look at your bank balance you realise that you haven't made any money from the project. It's going way over schedule and it's costing you as much as you're making. They keep requesting more and more features and eventually you hate the project.

If this sounds familiar, email me michael@sellyourservice.co.uk. I'd love to hear your similar stories!

If you want to avoid this and experience a totally different method you need to decide your price first. You see, pricing a project *after* deciding what you're delivering leaves too much margin for error. There are too many variables. You don't know what your expenses will be; you don't know what could change or what you'll need to add. It also assumes that the customer is going to stick to their end of the bargain. How often have you heard "we need this done quickly. We're not afraid of hard work and we can get the content over to you" only to have them be the ones who hold the project up?

Finally, it puts the power of how much you earn and keep into the hands of the client. They have no idea how much money you need or want to make. You're letting their needs and required features and benefits dictate how much your business earns. That's like letting them decide what you can charge. Would you be happy with a customer telling you how much you should spend on your bills or business? Of course not! So why are you letting them decide how much you earn?

Instead, let's take control back and decide the price first. And the first part of this equation is to work out how much you want to earn. How much does your business need to make? Do you have a monthly or yearly goal? Do you have a budget? If not, you need to get one FAST. We'll talk more about how much money your business needs to earn and how much you personally need to live comfortably. Would £50,000 a year suit you? What are your monthly expenses? What are your yearly expenses? How much do you need to live on to be comfortable, or even secure? These questions will determine your price and how many customers you need to work with. As a rule of thumb, if you need to earn £50,000 a year your business will probably need to do around £100,000 a year in sales.

It's a rough guide, but it's accurate enough for our model here. £100K a year in sales is 4 x £25K customers. That's one customer every 4 months. Or four customers a year. Doesn't that sound way easier than searching for dozens of customers who pay less? This is why we need to work out our price first because what we decide to charge, determines the rest of our entire customer acquisition process. Before we go on, I need you to have five **monthly** numbers clearly defined in your head:

1. How much do you personally require each **month** to live as you are now? This is your standard income level. Write it out below.
2. What is the bare minimum that you require each month, just to survive? This is your survival level income. Write it out below. It should be lower than your standard income level.
3. How much do you require to live comfortably? This is your standard level income plus additional items that you would like to see regularly. Think savings, holidays, houses etc. It will be roughly 50% - 100% more than your standard income level i.e standard income level x 1.5. Write that below.
4. How much do you require to be financially secure? This is a level where your expenses are taken care of and you're able to save regularly. This will be roughly 150% of your comfort level income. Write it below.
5. How much do you require to be financially free? This is where your bills, expenses and additional security finances are taken care of each month. You no longer have to work every day and you can do what you want, when you want, how you want and with whom you want. This is usually 300% of your financially secure number. Write it below.

Once you've got those numbers, I want you to look at your financially free monthly costs. That's the highest number you wrote. Whatever that figure is per month, multiply it by 12 and that's your ideal yearly target. Find your last project invoice and work out how many of those customers would you need to achieve that number? Can you imagine working on that many projects?

How many £25,000 marketing funnel projects do you need to fulfil that number? Is it fewer than your previous project level? How many five figure projects would you need to reach your comfort or security level? It's probably fewer customers still. This is why we look at price first because now we're in control of how many customers we work with.

However you feel about £25,000, we're going to start at that number and we decide the price first. Or, if you need to, we could look at £75,000 or £120,000 price tags. The price is irrelevant as long as it's at least five figures, more than 150% of your last invoice and makes you a little bit queasy at the sight of it. Throughout the rest of the book I'm going to show you how to attract clients that have that budget, how to sell to them, close them and avoid them saying "can you do it cheaper?"

£25K Drop

In order to raise our prices and define our price first, I use an exercise called the £25K Drop. This was taught to me by my sales coach Sean Mize and has never steered me wrong. It's the fastest method I know to set a price first and make sure you're profitable. As much as customers might not like to admit it, what you deliver isn't up to them. It's up to you. You're the expert. Even if you might not think you're the expert at the moment (which we'll get onto), you are. Reiterating what we've talked about previously, you need to determine the price first. That's the fastest way to boost your revenue and also to begin separating yourself from every other supplier and marketer out there. Everyone else lets the customer tell them what they should do and that the marketer should come back with a price. That's what amateurs do. It's not what Five Figure Funnel Builders do. It's not what experts do. What experts do is set the price and tell the customer what they'll get. If it doesn't suit that customer, then fine, move on.

Experts have obviously done this so many times that they know exactly what the price is. Only someone with experience and practice would determine the price first. At least that's the perception. In fact, it follows the other way around. Determining the price first allows you to decide what the experience is that you're delivering. Here's how the £25K Drop works. I'm going to give you £25,000 tomorrow and I want results. It's as simple as that. When you wake up you'll be £25,000 richer, and deposited into your bank account will be that exact amount. I don't care if you've never had a project this big before; I don't care that you don't know what I'm giving you the money for; I just know I have a budget of £25,000 and I want your help. I've heard you're good and that you can get my business results.

After seeing that sum in your account, you can't give it back, you can't refund it, you have to give me something in return. That's the relationship you need to start thinking about with your customer. They're going to give you £25,000; you're going to give them something in return. OK. Let's slow down a little and wind back. £25,000 might sound like a lot, but it really isn't. If you're already thinking that you eat £25,000 projects for breakfast, then I'm giving you £250,000 or £2.5 million. It should be a price that makes you nervous and a little uncomfortable.

As a good rule of thumb it should always be AT LEAST 150% of your previous project price, or if you've sold 10 x £2500 products you should be looking for 1 x £25,000 project. If you've never charged £25,000 before I want you to use that number. That's the absolute minimum. What we're doing is forcing ourselves to stop thinking "How much can I charge for this service or product?" and more "How much value and what can I deliver for this cost?" Here's why this question is so important. Back when I first started selling, designing and building marketing funnels, I jumped the gun with a huge customer and talked myself into a £60,000 (roughly $100,000 at the time) contract. I had literally never seen that type of money before, especially through my business. It turns out that the customer needed a marketing funnel designed, built and managed. I was someone who could do that.

The crazy part is that they asked ME if £60,000 was enough. Essentially that was their budget, they were reaching the end of the financial year and they wanted £60,000's worth of results. Gladly, I accepted the budget and said I'd get back to them with a proposal. Walking back to my car (sweating) I thought that day I would finally be revealed as a conman (imposter syndrome). "Today is the day people see that I have no idea what I'm doing" I thought.

I got back to my office and immediately called up my business partner. I asked him "What the hell am I going to do? What am I going to say I can do for sixty grand!?" His answer was blindingly simple "Well you'd better deliver them 60 grand's worth of value." That might sound overly simple, but I was trying to over complicate things. I simply made a list of things that I thought would be included in a sixty-thousand-pound project. I forced myself to list off things that sounded like they belonged in a project of that size:

- A website
- Email lead capture automation
- Content ideas for traffic attraction
- Lead magnet content ideas
- Landing page copy
- Email marketing copy
- Marketing funnel design
- Marketing automation trigger design (when to send an email and how often etc.)
- Face to face consultation
- Dedicated coaching every week

I then dug a little deeper and asked myself "If I had another business approach me for the same project, what would I offer them? Would I offer the same stuff? Or because I can only be at one place at a time, would I change the offer slightly?"

So I started to list things that I could offer, inside the £60,000 package that wouldn't need me:

- Reporting automation (traffic, subscribers, conversions and sales)
- Paid traffic opportunities and identification (I could pay a student to create new audience profiles on Facebook to explore new traffic opportunities)
- Subscription product creation (creating recurring revenue for my customer)
- Project management lists, sent to my customer's staff so they knew what they were doing this month

- Access to all notes, recordings and presentations for their and other customers coaching sessions.

Eventually, I had a big old list of stuff that I felt was worth £60,000. Then I saw a Facebook post that almost caused me to call the whole thing off. The same customer put the project out to tender and was asking around for other people to get in touch. I saw it both on their Facebook page and it was posted in a couple of digital marketing groups. I knew it. I knew it was too good to be true. They wanted to go out to tender? They obviously thought I wasn't up to the task. I was angry (with hindsight, I now totally see that they pretty much had to go to tender and I was foolish to get angry – but hey, I was younger then!) In fact, I was so angry that I made changes to the proposal mere hours before I was going to send it. I was so sure that I wouldn't get the project, I was going to *not* get the project on my terms. As well as remove things, I started listing what they don't get in the project:

- No website – I'll just advise on what your current site needs to do. If you want a new site, that's a new project
- I don't build anything, I'm happy to design and give you those funnel designs and then teach your staff how to build, but I don't build
- I don't buy, pay for or manage the CRM and marketing automation system. That's your technology and responsibility
- If you're paying for traffic, that's your budget

All of a sudden, I started to feel that I could easily advise and consult this business to build and manage their own marketing automation funnels. I wouldn't be supporting or building anything myself and I could consistently improve and add value to the project by keeping myself up to date and educated. Finally, I handed over the proposal and wouldn't you know it (bearing in mind I was literally positive that I wouldn't get it), they went for it.

Customer: "When can you start?"

Me: "As soon as you pay the deposit and book out a week to start the coaching"

Customer: "Cool, the money should be with you by this afternoon"

Me: 😊

After all that, they went for it. They wanted me to consult and coach. Not build and support. They were paying staff to do that. They needed someone to take ownership of the process and get it to work harder.

I wouldn't have ever come up with a monthly retainer product and service that cost £60,000 unless I was forced to. Now, the first stage of my coaching and consultation is forcing customers and businesses to dream of a product bigger than they've ever delivered before. That's what we're going to do now. Take a piece of paper, or use the worksheet coming up and write £25,000 at the top. You now need to list out what you are going to deliver to the customer. For example:

- Sales page
    - o Copy
    - o Design
    - o Build
- Webinar sign up page
    - o Copy
    - o Design
    - o Build
    - o Reminder emails
- Webinar thank you page
    - o Copy
    - o Design
    - o Build
- CRM integration for optin forms, webinar sign ups and sales
- Optin forms
    - o 3 optins across website for a lead magnet
- Thank you page for optins
    - o One page for all 3 - generic optin page
- Sales emails
    - o 12 part sales campaign
- Follow up emails
    - o Post webinar reminders
- Automated weekly report
    - o New leads
    - o Conversions
    - o Sales
    - o Traffic
- Fortnightly call for the duration of the project
- Dedicated support email address

You don't have to know how to build a CRM system. You don't have to worry about conversion reports and audits. You just think "what would I deliver to someone if they were going to give me £25,000?"

What would the customer get? What would you offer? How can you provide X value for Y investment? Write out an exhaustive list of everything you would give someone if they handed you a five figure sum. Would you deliver that to everyone?

This process doesn't need to rely on you building and delivering the work.

We'll see in a later chapter how to create leverage and allow others to do the heavy lifting for you. You've done the hard work already, you've attracted the customer. Let someone else do the tactical work. Also, this isn't set in stone. Just brainstorm, let your imagination run wild. If someone gave you £25K, what would you give them? What *don't* they get? What's excluded? Think of what you could offer if someone forced you to deliver a £25K project. What would you offer? What wouldn't you offer? Could you easily scale that product and serve it to 10 people a day or would you need to be at every consultation?

Give each dollar a job

If we start with our price first, it's easy to get carried away when thinking of products and services that we could deliver to the customer. "For £25,000 I could do AMAZING things for a client!"

But we have to remember to stay profitable and scalable. The biggest trap that marketing service businesses fall into, is not knowing where their money is going before they receive it. Have you ever had an invoice get paid by your customer and at first thought "Awesome! I'm glad this has come in!" only in a few weeks or even days later to think "Where the hell did all that money go?"

Now tell me, have you ever thought that the solution to this problem would be more money? Or a bigger project budget? If only you had a windfall sum like £25,000 land in your account, then you'd be set right? One big payment would seriously help your business maybe?

Unfortunately, it won't. The 'lottery win' style of financial management isn't very effective. Up to 1/3rd of lottery winners in the US go bankrupt[2] and lottery winners declare bankruptcy 3-5 times faster than the average person[3].

You might think that £25,000 will fix your problems, or that £1 million would be the solution to everything. But what happens is that we don't manage larger sums of money better if we're not managing smaller sums first. A large windfall of five figures might sound like it'll solve your problems, but history, data and a little imagination will quickly prove that we wouldn't be better off. It's like walking through the desert, dying of thirst, desperate for a glass of water, but instead of a smaller manageable quantity of water in a glass, we have gallons dumped onto us at once. Unless we have a way to capture, keep and use that water, it'll disappear into the sand.

---

[2] https://wolfstreet.com/2018/04/17/nearly-one-third-of-u-s-lottery-winners-declare-bankruptcy/
[3]
https://www.mitpressjournals.org/doi/abs/10.1162/REST_a_00114#.VpLMM1J327Q

The key to making sure that your pricing really does help your business, is deciding what you're going to do with every dollar before it hits your account. We're building water storage for the rain, not just praying for more rain. Yes, in most cases I believe that marketing businesses and funnel builders *do* need to raise their prices, but it's only half the story. You have to be prepared to manage the money that comes in, rather than just hope for more money. This isn't a case of having more, it's a case of keeping more. One of the most universal truths of money is that it flows faster and in greater quantities to those that know how to manage it. When you decide what each dollar is going to do, before it even hits your account, you're demonstrating that you can handle greater and greater quantities of money.

Here's how to give each dollar a job

Full disclosure, this method is worked from the Mike Michalowicz model of Profit First, which I highly recommend you read. But for the purposes of our business I've changed some of the details and simplified the application. The concept is that for every £1 or £100 or £10,000 that comes in, we know exactly where each dollar goes. We'll use percentages to allocate money for tax, paying ourselves, paying suppliers and contractors, business overheads and keeping some aside for profit. Up to roughly £250,000 a year we want to split our income into four areas.

- Profit
- Paying ourselves
- Paying the tax man
- Paying the business

Most people believe that
$$profit = income - expenses$$
But the true equation for profit is
$$expenses = income - profit$$

You must allocate profit first (good title for a book), and work backwards. Mike Michalowicz, Robert Kiyosaki, George Clason, Tony Robbins, Warren Buffett, Napoleon Hill and many other financial experts know this is the case.

When you begin to split your income into these four areas, it changes the perception of price and what you'll deliver to the customer. After you've gone through this exercise, go through the £25K Drop again and see if you want to cut back on some of the features. You might realise that you can't afford to deliver everything you thought. For every dollar that comes in, a certain percentage is going to be split into one of these four areas.

- 50% for paying ourselves
- 30% for paying the business
- 15% for paying the tax man
- 5% for profit

This means for every £100 that comes in, it looks roughly like this
.

- £50 for paying ourselves
- £30 for paying the business
- £15 for paying the tax man
- £5 for profit

Did I mention that we'll be paying ourselves for the work? As the business owner it's vital that you pay yourself. In fact, for a £25,000 project, you might be paying yourself more than when you were charging less and keeping more of it yourself. For a £25,000 project, the pricings work out to be the below.

- £12,500 for paying ourselves
- £7500 for paying the business
- £3750 for paying the tax man
- £1250 for profit

Look at these four points very carefully. This is your pricing structure. This is giving every dollar a job. And up to around £250,000 in revenue per year, these percentages will stay the same. For each £25,000 project, 30% or £7500 will go to business expenses.

What are business expenses? These are your overheads and project costs. If your office rent is £300 a month and your VA costs you £600 a month, combined with a few other costs like email automation and hosting, you might have a monthly overhead of £1500. These are your costs to the business that you'd have to pay even if you didn't make any money. If you made no sales, you'd still have to pay these costs; these are your overheads.

Project costs are expenses that you pay when you take on a new project. It's essentially your budget for working with the customer. With overheads of £1500, that leaves £6000 for project costs, assuming the project only takes a month. If the project takes two months, that leaves you with £4500 for project costs as your monthly overheads of £1500 obviously occur twice in a two month period. When we get onto the chapter about creating leverage with products, you'll see how you can make sure that projects don't run over or cost you more than they should.

With new projects, I like to work backwards from my project costs. If we're looking at a new project for a customer, I'll list out all the features I think they need and I'll ask myself "How much would this cost me to hire someone else to do it?" I could hire someone part time; I could outsource it; I could take people on per project. There isn't a right or a wrong way, but if we start off thinking that each project will take about three months, that allows us four £25,000 projects per year which equals £100,000 revenue. Where you are right now with low or no capital to invest in hiring, it might make more sense to allocate £2500 of that project price to pay someone else to do the work.

In the chapter on creating leverage with products, you'll see how we'll create standardised documents and protocols to allow hires and people you take on to execute the job to a high standard, without you doing the work. At the moment, we want to focus on pricing.

Immediately, you might be looking at that 50% to pay for yourself and think "Why can't I just do the work and keep the 30% in the business?" Think about how hard and awkward it is to attract a customer and make a sale. That's the hard part and the most vital part of running a business. You as the owner are taking 100% of the risk and you're the one who's set up the business. You absolutely should be rewarded for attracting a customer and making a sale. Delivering the work is the easy part. Here's a list of things you've had to do to win that client:

- Create a product
- Set up a payment system and take a payment
- Set up a bank account
- Possibly apply for a loan
- Write a proposal
- Meet the customer and qualify them
- Understand their needs
- Present a solution
- Turn your back on traditional income
- Sell the product
- Close the customer
- Overturn objections
- Answer questions
- Reply to emails
- Cold call and prospect
- Generate the leads
- Nurture prospects
- Show that you're capable and willing to deliver the product
- Develop a relationship with the customer
- Attend networks and business functions

- Build a business and brand

That's a lot of work and you deserve to be rewarded for that. And that's not even the end of it because you need to do that every single time you want a new client. Luckily, it gets easier and faster and luckily, you're reading a book that's going to help you do just that. Nevertheless, delivering the work to the client is NOT your primary goal when you're running your funnel business - your primary goal is **selling marketing funnels**.

When you pass the work over to your team and hires, they'll build the project. Don't worry about that because when they're building, you've plenty of other things to do. You need to repeat that list above and do more. See the list below:

- Attend business growth seminars
- Read books
- Listen to podcasts
- Ask for referrals
- Create content
- Work on your status as an authority
- Be interviewed
- Promote the business
- Promote your products
- Sell to more people
- Manage staff
- Manage suppliers
- Cut back on costs
- Grow and scale the business
- Think of new product ideas
- Think of new sales strategies
- Acquire and research new markets

That's not even including the everyday human activities that you need to do just to survive. You're going to hire some great people. You're going to hire some duds and lazy people, but overall, most people want to do good work. Let them do that. They don't want the risk of running a business. They just want to build funnels and you should let them.

"Why don't I cut back on my pay and give more to the business expense?" Another common question. If you're getting paid 50% of the project, why not make that less and give more money to other people?

Earlier in this section we talked about how money flows to those that prove they can manage it better. If you learn how to make more sales and standardise your process, eventually you'll be able to take less and less from each project and give more and more to the business. But right at the start, until you've reached around £250K in revenue, you need to pay yourself. DO NOT make the mistake of thinking you'll pay yourself later because you never will. Yes, the first few projects might be a bit clunky and you'll have to work out the finer details for the payment structure. But you will get there and eventually it'll be second nature. Your job as the business owner is to raise capital.

No business in history has ever gone under or failed because they focused on sales. No business has ever gone under because their products and services weren't perfect. No business has ever been considered unsuccessful because they have a really hard working owner who delivers the work. Your job is to run a business, let other people work in the business. We're lucky that we're going to be charging higher prices than before, so we can afford to hire people.

The last part of this exercise is to go over your £25K Drop exercises and re-evaluate it. Does what you've written down make sense for someone else to deliver? Don't worry if you think you're the only person who knows how to do it. Or if you don't know how to deliver it, just look over what you're potentially offering and ask yourself "What will it cost me to deliver this to a client? What will I have to pay to have someone or a team of people deliver this to a client?" It's OK to remove some features entirely or replace them. Remember, this is not a question of what you're being paid to deliver; it's a question of what you're paying other people to deliver.

Product menagerie

Product menagerie is one of my favourite terms. Aside from menagerie being one of my favourite words, after Tennessee Williams' book The Glass Menagerie. I think 'a collection of animals' is the best collective noun and descriptor for our suite of products.

Products have a life of their own. They have personalities and they thrive in different environments. We have to care for them and put them in the right eco-system for them to thrive. In many cases they can co-exist together in harmony. And in some cases they need to be kept apart, but in the same location, like a wildlife sanctuary.

You need to create a product menagerie and exhibit it to your customers, leads and audience. It's attractions that get people in and they'll want to learn more when they see how exciting they are and how they can help their business. Our product menagerie is made up of some vital components but there is a tiny caveat to what we're about to do.

During this exercise we're going to explore some lower prices. The temptation will be to focus on those lower prices to get customers in. The assumption is that it's easier to sell a cheaper product. The problem is that until you're comfortable selling your highest priced product, you'll struggle to sell all products. It takes just as much effort to sell a £25,000 marketing funnel as a £5000 marketing funnel. That list above of what we have to do to get each sale is the same for every product, so we might as well focus on a higher price.

On the other side, there is a misconception that I believe everyone should sell products at £25K+ which is a gross misunderstanding of what I've taught and said. What I have said is that you should be selling your marketing funnels for a minimum of £25K because that's what you're already building. You're building £25K funnels, you're just not charging £25K. There is nothing wrong with charging £2000 for a £2000 product, but anything under five figures that requires you to do or deliver the work, isn't profitable.

If a customer *does* say "We don't have £25,000, we only have £10,000" that's fine too. We'll sell them a £10,000 product. But we will not sell them a £25,000 product and charge them £10,000. The key to this exercise is to have every product remain profitable for you and valuable for the client. I'll show you how to deal with customers that say "That's too expensive" later, but we probably won't get that many customers who can't afford you in the first place. Yes, some people will always think you're expensive - your competitors, your audience, your friends. Some people are always going to think that you're charging crazy money. Let them. They've got zero interest in helping you build a profitable and scalable business. What they're really saying is "I don't think that *I* could ever deliver that much value, so surely no one else can?"

Take a piece of paper and write your £25,000 price at the top. Now, list out everything you're going to deliver for that price. Remember to remove or replace things that you don't think you can afford to pay others to deliver for you. This is your flagship product and the core offer that you'll be bringing to market.

Now I want you to write out £10,000 and ask yourself "If someone didn't have £25,000 but they did have £10,000 what would I remove from my £25,000 product and deliver to the customer? What would I replace or keep? Would some things be reduced or minimised?" Remember that a £10,000 project is roughly £3300 in expenses. For example in my £25,000 product I had the below:

- Sales page
  - Copy
  - Design
  - Build
- Webinar sign up page
  - Copy
  - Design
  - Build

- o   Reminder emails
- Webinar Confirmation page
  - o   Copy
  - o   Design
  - o   Build
- CRM integration for optin forms, webinar sign ups and sales
- Optin forms
  - o   3 optins across website for a lead magnet
- Thank you page for optins
  - o   One page for all 3 - generic optin page
- Sales emails
  - o   12 part sales campaign
- Follow up emails
  - o   Post webinar reminders
- Emails uploaded into email autoresponder and set to send
- Automated weekly report
  - o   New leads
  - o   Conversions
  - o   Sales
  - o   Traffic
- Fortnightly call for the duration of the project
- Dedicated support email address

If someone had less than half that budget, what would I offer them? Well, I'd remove a few things and keep some others. They wouldn't get me writing the copy for the sales pages, webinar page or thank you pages. Instead, we'd hold a 2 day copy-workshop and they can send the copy. We'll build the pages instead. They also don't get optin forms across the site. My new £10,000 product looks like the below:

- Sales page
  - o   Design
  - o   Build
- Webinar sign up page
  - o   Design
  - o   Build
  - o   Reminder emails
- Webinar thank you page
  - o   Design
  - o   Build
- CRM integration for optin forms, webinar sign ups and sales
- 2 day copy-writing workshop

- o   Sales page
- o   Webinar sign up
- o   Confirmation page
- o   Optin forms
- o   Thank you pages
- Sales emails
  - o   12 part sales campaign
- Follow up emails
  - o   Post webinar reminders
- Automated weekly report
  - o   New leads
  - o   Conversions
  - o   Sales
  - o   Traffic
- Fortnightly call for the duration of the project
- Dedicated support email address

I've removed items that are expensive and time consuming. However, they're still getting the same result. The goal is to help this customer generate sales via a webinar. £25,000 will get us to do the majority of the work. £10,000 means the customer has to do more of the work.

Customers want results. The size of their investment determines the speed, ease and level of work they need to commit. If they want it faster, great! They just need to pay for it. If they want it to be easier and less work on their behalf or if they want the result practically automated, awesome! That'll just cost them more.

When you focus on the result that the customer is getting, it's easier to set different price points. Customers can never ever complain about the price when you're offering them the result they want. *How* they get that result is entirely up to them. If they want you to write the copy you're more than willing to do that, but they'll have to pay for it.

"My nephew says he can do it for £500!" Ah yes, the ultra smart nephew who's good with computers, or the guy down the road at the business networking event who says anything over £1000 is a ripoff. Look, these people exist and yes, some customers will try to hammer you on price. It's not a question of learning how to handle them or sell to them. It's a question of rising above those customers and never letting them come near you. By the time you're done, you won't need to answer these questions because you'll stop hearing them.

We've now got a £10,000 product. I want you to do the same thing but with a £5000 price tag. Take your initial £25,000 and the £10,000 version and strip back the price and ask again "What do I keep and what do I get rid of?" Think of the following pricing brackets:

- £25,000
- £10,000
- £5000
- £3000
- £297 per month
- £97 per month
- £97
- £19
- £9

For example, I design and manage massive enterprise-level marketing funnels for roughly £30,000 a year. But for one-off payments of £97 people can buy the blueprint and architecture of a funnel to use on their own business (I even offer specific funnels for various businesses e.g. memberships, e-commerce, sports coaches etc.).

Think outside of the usual results and delivery processes. Results ≠ delivery. There is no *one* way to get some one results especially if they can't afford the £25,000 product. There are many ways to deliver results to people:

- Books
- Outsourcing
- Courses
- Templates
- Software
- Podcasts
- Audio training
- Training

Don't stick to traditional delivery models. Let's take this book: my goal is to help you sell a marketing funnel for £25,000. However, I also have a course at $1497USD and monthly coaching at $197USD per month. As well as personal one-on-one coaching for £25,000. All my products are designed to help you attract and close five figure deals. For some people the price is fine at $1497 for a course; for others, they want the book first.

List out your product menagerie with what you'd deliver for each price point. We're not going to sell every one of these products, but we are going to pick 3 or 4 and create a sales offer suitable for your market, as well as create expert positioning for you.

Summary

- Your price is your price - the market doesn't dictate it, you have to justify it though
- £25,000 is no more profitable than £19 if you don't know what you're delivering
- Set the price first and decide what you can afford to deliver
- You absolutely can be flexible on pricing if you're firm on deliverables

ASSETS

When funnel businesses struggle to scale it's not because of a lack of ambition, or dedication or willing to work hard. If we look at both sales and lead generation as the visible symptoms that show a lack of growth, it's usually the assets that the business has which prevents those metrics from growing. In this chapter we're going to create scalable assets that grow with your business and enable growth.

Standardise your product

One of the biggest reasons that marketing agencies struggle with productivity, profit and finding consistent work, is their inability to standardise their offer. As creative agencies and human beings, we tend to overvalue novelty. What this means is that we think each customer will want a totally bespoke and unique solution for their problems. It's as if for each new project we are expected to develop a brand-new solution, specific to their business and needs. You might think that your customers want bespoke and custom when in reality they don't.

They do want a solution that fits them, their needs and their business. They also want to feel like they are buying the right solution. However, buying the right solution and creating a bespoke solution are not always the same thing. For too long, marketing agencies and creative agencies have built bespoke solutions for customers and struggled with delivering the work and getting results for customers. Your job is to standardise an offer towards your niche. Going to market with an attitude of "I'll do whatever you need as long as you pay me" is only going to yield mediocre results. It also puts a cap on your income potential as that attitude tends to lend itself to a consultant or pay-per-hour approach. If you're the only person delivering results to the customer, they're buying your time and you'll never find the time or energy to work on your business. While we might think that customers either want to work with you or want a bespoke solution, it's usually not the case.

Customers that do insist on working with you are welcome to, if they can afford your much, much higher one on one fee.

Earlier, we chose a price that we were going to aim for. And we chose a part of the funnel process that we would deliver to the customer for that price. We then looked at a suitable niche for our business and defined who we're going after. The key now is to go back to our initial £25K Drop list of deliverables and work out what the standardised process is that we'll deliver to customers. Let's take our earlier £25K Drop example of a webinar sales funnel:

- Sales page
  o Copy
  o Design
  o Build
- Webinar sign up page
  o Copy
  o Design
  o Build
  o Reminder emails
- Webinar thank you page
  o Copy
  o Design
  o Build
- CRM integration for optin forms, webinar sign ups and sales
- Optin forms
  o 3 optins across website for a lead magnet
- Thank you page for optins
  o One page for all 3 - generic optin page
- Sales emails
  o 12 part sales campaign
- Follow up emails
  o Post webinar reminders
- Automated weekly report
  o New leads
  o Conversions
  o Sales
  o Traffic
- Fortnightly call for the duration of the project
- Dedicated support email address

The niche that we're going after is authors/speakers who are releasing a course to their current email list. A sales webinar funnel would suit them down to the ground. They'd need to have an active list, a CRM system and the time to build the webinar with us, as well as present it. This would be a perfect solution for authors/speakers looking to release a course to their current email list.

If I had £25,000 coming in to deliver this funnel project to a customer, I want to make sure I had templates and systems for as much as possible because it creates leverage for me and the business. Firstly, I'd have standardised lead qualification and discovery call scripts. If I'm asking the same types of people the same questions, I can get someone else to run those initial calls. It also means that I'll have similar standardised answers from the discovery and lead qualification calls which I can use in my proposal. If I have standard questions and answers, I can use them in my standardised proposal template.

During delivery, we'll also have a process and templates for all the bullet points above. Page design, webinar scripts, follow up emails. The more documentation we have, the faster we can do work for clients and it means I can hire people because they'll have a process they can follow. If they're following a documented process it means they're less likely to make mistakes and the margin for error is smaller. Standardising your process for delivery is critical to your business scaling and becoming profitable. It's also important that we know what we're selling every single time to customers. When we deliver bespoke solutions to every new customer, we're losing momentum in the niche and market that we've chosen. When we have a standardised product, our job becomes finding the right clients rather than delivering the most unique solution. Unique solutions sound attractive, but they're not as profitable. If you sell cars, do you completely build from scratch a new car each and every time? Of course not. The job is finding someone who is suitable for that car NOT building a bespoke suitable car for anyone and everyone.

Finally, we need a standardised system for attracting and converting clients. It's true that all the processes and systems and documentation in the world will help you deliver work to customers, but it won't necessarily help you *sell* funnels to your clients. The transition from marketing/sales to operations and delivery is critical and one must come before the other. You must have a standardised, scalable and repeatable sales process in order to make the best use of your standardised, scalable and repeatable delivery process. With a standardised delivery process or product, we can determine the benefits and future that our product provides. With a standardised sales process, we can repeatedly attract sales and leads.

What's the end result or transformation?

Let's start with the transformation that people are going to accomplish in order to reach their better future. You have a niche, in our case authors/speakers who are releasing a course to their current email list. At the moment they're in a negative state. They don't know what to do and how to get to a desired result. The result is a successful course product launched to their email list with lots of happy customers. What is your niche's happy, better, brighter future? This is where we'll want to do some creative writing. As counter intuitive as it sounds, customers will buy marketing funnels from you for very illogical and emotional reasons. People buy emotions and futures. We're selling futures, not features. Benefits are better futures. Your customer doesn't really care how you do something, they care about what *they* get out of it. Remember WIIFM? (what's in it for me?) That's all the customer is interested in. Deep down, they're not even too concerned about what you do for their business. They care about how you'll affect their life.

When we advertise gyms and diets, do we show pictures of gym equipment, vegetables and sweaty towels? No of course we don't. We show slim, healthy and fit people with massive smiles. We show them laughing and having fun with family. We show and sell the result and transformation. What does one of your customers look like when they've got everything they can from you? If you knock it out of the park, how does their morning look? How do other people see them? How do they see themselves? What's the positive, better future of themselves doing, saying, seeing, feeling and experiencing? Weak futures are where we say "In the future, my customer has more leads and sales" or "In the future my customer has a marketing automation system". Strong futures say "In the future, my customers wake up and have a lay in, knowing that they don't have to rush off to work. They can spend a little more time with their spouse and kids. When they walk into the office, they don't check their emails, instead, they look at their Stripe account and see more sales for their course even though last night, instead of working on sales campaigns and closing customers, they went for dinner with a friend."

"Strong futures make strong sales"

Strong futures make strong sales. The clearer we can make that future and the more enthusiasm we show for helping people get to that future, the easier we'll find selling. Even complex marketing systems and boring automation processes can have massive emotional benefits to customers.

Let's write out a series of better, brighter futures that your customer wants and would find desirable. This is the transformation that we're selling and the start of creating a scalable repeatable process. You can either answer these questions on a piece of paper or head to sellyourservice.co.uk/fivefigurefunnels and download our free worksheet. We want to get really detailed, bordering on creative writing. We want to build a desirable image in our mind of a customer who has totally transformed and is now living a happier, better life.

In the future, after working with me, my customers have...

This is the easy question. What does the customer have after working with you? Do they have a sales process? Email automation? Do they have more leads or sales? Do they have better conversion rates?

These are weak questions, but are a good place to start. Most funnel businesses will just answer these questions and then stop. You can look at the results or deliverables they want or what you give. For example, with our niche of authors/speakers who are releasing a course to their current email list, they'll have a successful course launch or more course sales or more customers on their email list. Write out as many things as you can think for what a customer will have, after they work with you.

In the future, after working with me, my customers feel...

This is where we start getting stronger futures that we can sell. How do your customers feel after working with you and what do they feel positively about? This isn't just about the product or service. It's not about how they feel about working with you. This is about their life and day and business. This is asking them how they feel about their experiences or how their life is better.

For example, they could feel relieved that they don't have to chase customers for invoices. They could feel excited to launch a new product. They could feel confident about their business. They feel proud to spend time with their kids in the morning. They feel confident in their team and what they're building.

Sales is a transference of enthusiasm. That's as complex as it needs to get. The more enthusiastic you are and the easier you make it for the customer to be enthusiastic, the more likely they are to buy. If you tell them of a future that they want and desire, you need to be enthusiastic about that future. Enthusiasm is an emotion, so be emotional! Describe the feelings and emotions that customers will experience after working with you.

What does your customer's average day look like when they work with you?

When your customer wakes up, what do they feel? What's the first thing they do? After working with you, what would the best possible morning be for that customer? For me, when I took on my business coach, my mornings were filled with potential. I found getting up in the morning easier because I couldn't wait to start work. I also woke up easier because I was sleeping better. Your customers have a day-to-day that they wish was different. Most people want something else from the 24 hours we have per day. They want to do other things, see other things, be with other people, travel, eat, listen, play and learn. This is a more literal future that you're creating. We're writing out the better, happier version of their day.

What does breakfast look like? What does their morning commute look like and how has it changed? What is their working day like and how is it better? What kinds of meetings, calls and opportunities are they seeing now? What does their inbox look like now? Draw a timeline of 6am to 10pm and walk through each step of their day, pointing out events that happen and how great they are for the customer.

How does the customer see themselves after working with you?

Status is a huge part of the buying process and when we remove all the sales talk, copy, benefits and features, what people are really buying is a better future version of themselves. Our internal status is typically the strongest vision we have of ourselves and is often what motivates us to make a change and buy something. So after someone has worked with you, what would they say about themselves? How is their own self-image improved or changed? Do they see themselves as a more confident business owner? Are they now a better husband and father? Do they call themselves a successful business owner and full time Mum? If you can understand that status transformation that someone wants to have, you'll find it much easier to sell marketing services. And make no mistake, your marketing funnels are absolutely capable of bringing that change to people.

What is a core, moral belief that they feel is good and that they've contributed to?

We are defined by our beliefs even to the point of taking our beliefs for granted. We act them out every minute of the day and make all our decisions based around what we believe. This 'belief definition' is so strong that almost every product on the planet has a moral argument either for or against it. People connect to those beliefs before they connect to the product. We search for things that bolster and define our beliefs rather than search for products and change our beliefs around them. If you strongly believe that electric cars are the future and will save the planet, you're more likely to buy an electric car. If you believe that your current financial status doesn't allow you to buy a brand-new electric car, you'll settle for a second hand electric car. Our moral 'good versus evil' beliefs are what define all the actions we take and it's something you need to deliver if you want to create truly transformational products. For example, I believe that if you are good at sales you're morally a better person. It's important for business owners to be both good at sales and love selling to their audience. Therefore, I create products that help people become good at sales and enjoy selling. The moral belief that my audience subscribes to is also that they should sell and be good at selling.

What are they afraid of if they don't do something? Or if they get it wrong?

Finally, I want to look at what they're afraid of if they don't change. This is the consequence of not transforming. It's the customer's inner fears and worries that drive them to take action today. If their beliefs, desires and wants are *why* people buy, their fears are *when* they buy. Their fears determine how quickly they'll take action. Think about the negative consequences that someone will face if they don't transform. Or, what happens if they try to transform and fail? What happens if they get it wrong? These internal fears are an important part of your final transformation. Their fear could be that they miss out of the best years of their child's early life. Or it could be that they'll never be financially successful. Maybe they're afraid of letting their parents down or their employees. Fear is the 'enemy'. It's the antagonist in their transformation and often the catalyst for desiring transformation in the first place. It might be that their fear is staying in the same place E.g. no change. Or it might be that they're afraid of something happening in the future.

Once you have multiple future descriptions, you have your transformation. This is the end of the journey and the end result your customer is looking for. What we've described is what customers are buying. It is now a case of putting all those notes into a final transformation. For example, with our authors releasing a course, take the below:

After working with us, our customers wake up and don't check their emails. They head out to the gym and come back to have breakfast with their family. They feel excited to start the day and get to the office knowing that they'll be working on important big picture stuff, rather than admin and fighting fires. Our customers arrive at their office and start writing their next book, before taking some time away from their desk to enjoy a proper lunch. Each day they see more course sales come in, delivered and processed without them chasing customers. By the end of the day they've collected more leads that they're sure will convert into customers in good time. They can see their personal brand growing and more people looking to work with them. Over time, they attract high paid speaking opportunities and product partnerships. They were afraid of launching their course to crickets that no one would buy and they'd be seen as a failure. Previously, they'd tried to launch a course and it didn't work. This time, they've exceeded their initial launch target and now have an automated system to deliver and sell courses to clients, without taking up their time. Now, they can just focus on promoting the course, building an audience and growing their brand. Finally, they can leave the office earlier than they used to and pick up their partner. Tonight, they're going to the theatre and they'll have dinner beforehand comfortable and confident that they've done the best job possible and that tomorrow will bring more sales and leads.

If that future looks desirable that's because it is. That's what we're selling. Regardless of the tools, processes, systems, platforms and tactics we employ, we're selling a transformation. These are all benefits. This is the transformation and the better future we're building for our customers.

Where are they now?

Now we need to understand where the customer is *now*. How does their average day look like today? What do they feel and experience today and what is their physical and financial situation today? Using the same questions above, based around what they have or don't have, what their emotions are; how they feel and their average day; write out a summary of what they are experiencing now.

Rather than repeat the questions above I've got a quick reminder here, and I'll also ask you a few other questions to get you to describe the situation and life that the customer is currently facing:

- Right now, my customers don't have...
- Today my customer feels...
- Some frustrating things that happen to my customers in their average day-to-day are...
- My customer sees themselves at the moment as...
- A deeply held belief that my customer struggles with today is...

Some other questions we can ask to better understand our customers current status:

- What are my current customers feeling guilty about in regards to their current situation?
- What looming threat are they aware of and conscious of, but at the moment they are unable to avoid or change?
- What are my customers' top 3 problems they are facing today?
- What mistakes have my customers made which might not be entirely their fault?
- How do my customers make themselves feel better when they've had a bad day?
- What would cause them to have a bad day? Why do they need to make themselves feel better?

- What mistake did my customers make which seems to follow them around?

In order to understand how great the transformation is that we will be taking customers on, we have to have a clear idea of where they are now. The greater the gap between where they are now and where they'll end up, the more work involved, the higher the price we can charge. The greater the effort required to get from 0 to 100, the more valuable it is perceived. Helping someone run their first 5k, while a fantastic starting point, is not as great an effort as helping someone run their first marathon. Similarly, the transition from someone who can comfortably run a half marathon to someone to run a full marathon isn't as great as someone starting from scratch. That's not to say that incremental change isn't valuable and that people don't pay for the final (and in some cases the most difficult) 5% of the journey. But typically, when we go to the market with an offer, we want to make a radical transformation rather than help people who are currently on that journey or process.

This is often where a lot of businesses trip up; they're trying to iterate and make better processes that already exist rather than trying to change the transformational journey that the customer goes on. Marc Benioff, co-founder of Salesforce understood this when bringing his CRM to the market. He wasn't trying to make CRM software better, he was completely redefining the journey that people took to their customer relationship experience. Benioff didn't just make the transformation easier; he completely redefined the journey and changed the process that someone would go through in order to get to their destination. When you look at the start and end of the journey, you begin to understand the process that the customer will go on. It's not enough to provide people with a new type of product or a new feature; we have to help them transform into something which is desirable. This is another creative writing exercise, it allows you to both personify and solidify your customer. These 2 exercises by the way, the start and the finish, are in my opinion more powerful than a standard customer avatar.

The customer avatar, while extremely important to certain areas of a marketing strategy, often leaves out the human aspect of the story and fails to help us connect with a real person. If I write out a compelling before and after story and also a customer avatar worksheet, then shared both of them with people, the before and after story is far more likely to connect with them. It's also more likely to connect with me as the owner because I can begin to understand how that person thinks rather than a list of demographics and psychographics. I've written out an example 'before' story below.

Before working with us, the customers have fitful and unpleasant nights' sleep worrying about the failure and potential catastrophe of the course launch. They've spent thousands of dollars on marketing, PR and course creation, only to learn that none of that really is going to help them launch a course successfully. Before launching their course or even thinking about the course, they are working every night trying to get more books sold and published while taking on exhausting and time-consuming consulting work. They have irregular income through royalties and some consulting work rather than a repeat and regular income which puts stress on their marriage and their household bills. They consistently see other authors have successful and profitable online courses while they continue to try and find work elsewhere or rely on the measly book income. It feels more and more overwhelming that so many people are accelerating past them, even if these people's content and knowledge isn't as great. Someone once told them that the book is all they'll need to grow their brand, and now they are realising that they need a scalable product in order to capitalise on their new found expert status. They've got absolutely no idea where to look, and they feel confused at the number of options they have available to them in order to launch their course. Finally, they know how expensive a course launch can be, and they know how much work it will take to get to where they want.

What milestones do customers need?

Now that we understand our better future and transformation, we need to understand the milestones that customers will need to pass in order to reach that better future. The final transformation you're delivering to the customer will require them to pass multiple indicators that they are moving in the right direction. This is about feedback to both the customer and yourself that the project and the customer are making progress and beginning to transform. When we begin to understand what the milestones are that someone will accomplish, we begin breaking down the journey they'll be taking. This not only begins to solidify our offering, but it proves that we have a standardised process (which helps with authority) and also gives us a set of benefits which we can sell to the customer.

Let's start thinking about the journey and milestones that customers will need to pass in order to achieve the better transformation they desire. If you'd like an exercise worksheet to download for free, head to sellyourservice.co.uk/fivefigurefunnels or grab yourself a piece of paper and turn it landscape. On the left-hand side of the page write the word 'Start', and on the right hand side of the page write the word 'Finish'. The 'Finish' is where your customers are going to be after working with you. That's the best possible future and outcome. I want you to draw a line from the Start to the Finish and see your process and product as the timeline and link between the Start and the Finish. Underneath the word 'Finish', write out a few benefits and desirable futures that the customer will experience. They can just be bullet point summaries of the desirable end results or transformations from the exercise above. Similarly, with the Start end of the timeline, write out a few bullet points of where they are now. Again, if you'd like to see an example and a worksheet you can use head to sellyourservice.co.uk/fivefigurefunnels.

As with everything this is an iterative process. It requires you to write out a few different examples. You might go back and change your milestones depending on what you learn as things begin to mature and as you think over them. That's absolutely fine, we're not committing anything to concrete just yet. I'll give you all the frameworks and templates that I know of and eventually what we have is an extremely desirable product and offer which we can take to the market. It will also begin to give us a standardised operating procedure for delivering the product to the customer. Milestones are better for our products when they are considered progressive. If we think about the end result of transformation, the goal might be to run a marathon. The milestones in that case are not necessarily the literal milestones of run one mile, run 2 miles, run 3 miles etc. The milestones for a transformation to run a marathon in this case would be run your first 5k, run your first 10k, run your first 10 miles, run your first half marathon, run your first 20 miles, complete a marathon. Each milestone will have individual steps that break down that milestone further, but we are looking for progressions for the ultimate transformation. In your case, you'll want to look at the end result that the customer has and think about what they will need to have or pass, in order to begin reaching that future.

In many cases there is an obvious timeline to the milestones. For example, you tend to have to train for a 5k before you can take on a half marathon. Similarly with cooking, you need to do certain steps in order. For example, if we're making a cake we'll need to blend the ingredients together before putting it in the oven. However, there are non-linear milestones which could be checked off in any order. If we were creating a full marketing campaign for a new product for a customer, having a sales page, follow up process and social media ads might not necessarily go in a strict order. Don't worry too much about the order in general, for the time being we just want to list out the milestones that someone would have to pass and check off, in order to reach their better transformation. Ideally, we are looking for between 5 and 7 milestones for the customer. Milestones not only provide feedback that the customer is moving in the right direction but also give us building blocks for reaching that end result. Milestones might not necessarily be something that needs to be done or completed, they could be something that the customer has or achieves. In some cases such as the model for grief, each step in the process is a feeling or emotion. Denial, anger, bargaining, depression, acceptance, for example.

In our case we want to give a framework to customers for what they can both expect while going on the journey, as well as giving them an idea of what we're going to be working on. Most businesses will see these milestones as features and talk about how they're going to 1. build them a website 2. set up the CRM system 3. create the marketing copy etc. Instead, we're going to tell the customer what they need at each milestone they pass through which proves we are moving in the correct direction. So taking your piece of paper and starting on the left-hand side towards the Start, what is the first milestone that someone will need to pass or accomplish in order to begin reaching their transformation? What's the first thing they need to do or have, in order to start seeing progress? Try to think about moving out of their current state and just gaining some kind of momentum. For example with this book, in order to help you sell a £25,000 marketing funnel, the first step is in fact to help you define a niche that you want to go after. The milestone was that you need to have a niche you are willing to attract in order to start working towards a £25,000 marketing funnel project. If you've got a few 'first milestones' either accept that one of them will have to be first and the rest will come later, or ask yourself if all of those milestones are in fact a part of one large milestone.

There is no golden rule for how big a milestone should be. Remember, the greater the gap between the Start and the Finish the greater the value and therefore the price. It's also a case that in order to get an entire country out of Third World debt the milestones are things like 'completely reform the education process' or 'eliminate political corruption'. Each of those milestones in themselves will have a smaller set of milestones and so on and so forth. The larger the transformation you're offering might have multiple steps. Another good place to start is countering the common mistake or bad practice that people usually start with when attempting this journey. For example with losing weight, most people will go out and buy themselves a lot of new sports equipment. Your first milestone might be to write a mission statement instead. Just disrupt their initial idea of where they should be starting.

Also, remember to look at your £25K Drop exercise to remind you of the types of products and services you're going to include in your process. As we mentioned before, most funnel businesses fail because they don't standardise their product offering. The success of an offer is not defined by the process you take people on or the products you deliver to them, but the offer you create around that process. This is another classic case of selling benefits compared to features. The £25K Drop exercise shows us the features that we will be installing for customers. When we create a process for delivering those features, we're beginning to move towards benefits. Finally, by the end of this chapter you will see the benefits and sellable futures that your process and features will provide for your customers. Your £25K Drop exercise gives you the deliverables, but your offer is going to show people what they will have when they receive those deliverables. The offer is the illogical, emotional part and story that sells the product to the customer. In terms of sales sophistication, explaining the features and deliverables is level 1. Explaining the process is level 2, but the most sophisticated and effective technique (level 3) is explaining the offer. The process is a stage which many businesses including funnel builders, ignore, feeling it's too superfluous. However, it does multiple things as well as help standardise our offer and begin to create an offer for our customers.

For example with our author who is launching a course based on his second book, the first milestone that he needs to uncover in my opinion is testing his idea in the marketplace which we usually call an 'I need your help' campaign, or 'Shot across the bow' campaign. This is where we'll send an email out and social content to his group and email list, asking if they would be interested in learning more about the book's subject matter. The feedback that we get is usually a good indicator of how we should sell the course. Most people believe that the first step in order to sell a course is to build a course, and this is fundamentally incorrect. This is why my first milestone is to send an '*I need your help* campaign' or even better the first milestone is really 'Test the market'. We then move through the rest of the milestones. As a rule, as previously mentioned, you want to try and keep it between 5 and 7 milestones. This is not a hard and fast rule, but the evidence suggests that people are able to handle that many steps when having it explained to them. Anything more tends to be over complicated and a tad diluted (perhaps with unnecessary steps). Anything fewer and it is seen as too simple and not worth the transformation. What we're building here is the framework for our offer. It's the structure that our sales campaigns and pitches are going to be based around. We're only going to be selling something which we already know how to deliver. Write out the rest of your milestones and try to keep it between 5 and 7. Focusing on the core milestones will help you clarify your offering and begin to standardise your operating procedures. This also improves productivity and profitability. An example for our course launch milestones would be below.

1. Test the market
2. Create a sales webinar
3. Promote the sales webinar
4. Sell to webinar attendees and follow-up with attendees
5. Create one month, 15 email sequence launch campaign
6. Create 3 stage Facebook ads campaign
7. Appear on podcasts and create content to promote course

At the moment there is no model or acronym for this process. You can see that it's a pretty standard marketing campaign for a product of that type. It is essentially the steps that someone needs to take in order to reach that desired transformation. If they did all of those things, they would have a successful course launch. Of course, they can increase the likelihood that their course launch will be successful by following that process with me. Hopefully, this is also giving you some insight into how we're going to create content and sales letters going forward. Our process tells people what they need to do. Our free content and sales content tells people in greater detail what they are going to do and the benefits of what they'll do. When they buy from us we will tell them how to do it.

What steps do people need for each milestone?

Now we have our basic outline or framework for the product, we need to flesh out a little detail under each milestone. Each milestone might be considered a result that we need to achieve to drive someone to that in transformation. But each result needs to be made up of smaller steps or tasks to build that result. For each milestone you now need to write up the individual steps or tasks that someone needs to accomplish in order to achieve that milestone. For example, milestone one in the above example is 'Test the market'. This is also called a 'Shot across the bow' campaign or sometimes 'Initial outreach'. The name doesn't really matter in our case, but the tasks that need to be executed in order to mark that milestone off could be something like the below:

- Write a 5 part email campaign asking subscribers for help and ideas about problems or products that they would be interested in solving or seeing
- Create 2 or 3 Facebook posts with the same content asking for responses in the comments
- Schedule the email campaign to go out over a period of 2 weeks to your email list
- Collect and collate all responses
- Look for similarities in desired results, problems and language
- Reach back out to the market with a 3 part campaign asking "Would you be interested If I showed you how to [solve problem or achieve desired result]?"

As you can see these steps go into a little more detail and begin to give us some direction on how to achieve each milestone. Hopefully, you can also see how we would begin to create blog content around writing a 5 part campaign asking subscribers for help. Or create video content around how to understand what your customers want to buy. Eventually, you'll create processes and documentation for all of these individual tasks. Each task with its own smaller set of bullet points and directions. This is how we give standardised structure to our £25K Drop exercise, as well as how we begin to inform the desirable future offer that we will put out to the marketplace and our customers. Write out your individual steps per milestone. Another good number to aim for is roughly 6 steps per milestones. You don't have to go into hyper specific detail but enough detail that each step for each milestone could be understood without explaining too much. I've created an example process/standardised offer below with steps per milestone so you can see the level of detail that we use for each stage.

1. I need your help campaign
    a. Write a 5 part email campaign asking subscribers for help and ideas about problems or products that they would be interested in solving or seeing
    b. Create 2 or 3 Facebook posts with the same content asking for responses in the comments
    c. Schedule the email campaign to go out over a period of 2 weeks to your email list
    d. Collect and collate all responses
    e. Look for similarities in desired results, problems and language
    f. Reach back out to the market with a 3 part campaign asking "Would you be interested If I showed you how to [solve problem or achieve desired result]?"
2. Create a sales webinar
    a. Use the language, desired result and desired problems to solve as a topic for a sales webinar
    b. Outline 3 methods for solving the problem or achieving the desired result
    c. Create a product or offer to sell on the webinar at the end of the call
    d. Explain a myth or misconception that prevents people from achieving those results or solving those problems
    e. Include credibility and authority slides to explain who you are
    f. Make sure the content will be suitable for evergreen promotion
3. Promote the sales webinar
    a. Use the content from the webinar to create a squeeze page to collect leads for the live webinar call
    b. Use a confirmation page to measure conversions and confirm people are signed up as well as provide them with more dates and times as well as reminders and calendar links
    c. Provide a free download or gift if possible

     d.   Create a delivery page ahead of time with space to host the webinar replay as well as links to the offer and product

     e.   Create 8 part email campaign to promote the webinar

     f.   Create a reminder sequence to remind people who have signed up to the webinar

4. Sell to webinar attendees and follow-up with attendees

     a.   Pitch the products to webinar attendees tying the problems and results from the webinar content to similar problems, results and benefits on the product

     b.   Give people a call to action and signup link to purchase

     c.   Send a 1-2-3 email campaign to everyone who attended and send the replay to people who missed it

     d.   Promote the replay to those who didn't sign up

     e.   Automate the 1-2-3 follow up campaign to send to those who watch the replay

5. Create one month, 15 email sequence launch campaign

     a.   Write a 15 part email sequence sales campaign

     b.   Space out over 4 to 5 day periods and send to noncustomers and all leads

     c.   Create 3 sales pages with similar messaging and content displayed in different media e.g. sales letter, video sales letter and product page

     d.   Use the 15 part email sequence to promote the sales pages and the webinar sign up page

     e.   Put the webinar replay into evergreen mode and strip out dates from the squeeze page and thank you page

     f.   Automates the follow-up email sequence to leads to check out at least 2 sales pages

6. Create 3 stage Facebook ads campaign

     a.   Remarketing the webinar squeeze page to all traffic that visit the website

     b.   Remarketing the checkout and sales pages to all qualified leads and people who have visited the sales pages

     c.   Remarket at the sales page to those who watch the replay

7. Appear on podcasts and create content to promote course

     a.   Book podcasts to appear on as a guest to promote the course and potentially create an offer or affiliate deal with the interviewer

     b.   Turn the webinar into a killer content post and promote with links to the webinar or even an opt in form

     c.   Ask the list to promote the killer blog post and share on social media offer a free download or gift to the listeners of the podcast interviewer

As you can see some of these steps are slightly larger than others. For example 6.a is remarketing an entire webinar squeeze page to all traffic that visits the website. This of course is in itself its own mini milestone, with an entire ad campaign and custom audience built in Facebook. However, the singular benefit and point of that particular task is enough to give direction to people who are looking to launch their course. You'll also notice that despite having quite a specific niche, the process isn't necessarily specific to authors or courses. One of the biggest mistakes funnel builders and all businesses make is thinking their process has to be unique to their audience. In truth *this* book could be written for accountants, consultants, teachers or web developers.

The process of helping someone sell a product for £25,000 is no different for funnel builders than anyone else. However, my audience and trust and authority is built up within that particular market. You'll become known as someone who helps a particular audience, not as someone who delivers a particular process. Having a process and product works miracles especially for your authority and expertise levels. However, it's a question of working with the audience and delivering to them what they need, rather than trying to create a hyper specific niche product that only one type of customer wants to use. Don't over complicate it. If it works for your audience, fantastic. The offer and the benefits are what will sell it to that particular audience.

Create benefits from milestones

Here's where most funnel builders stop. They'll create a product and not turn that product into an offer. The product is what someone gets, the offer is what they buy. This is the equivalent to features being what people get and benefits being what people buy. I believe that benefits have been massively over-simplified by sales and marketing education. We're taught phrases like 'Sell the sizzle not the steak' or 'Sell the destination not the plane ticket'. These don't go far enough into what a benefit really is. A benefit is just a better future. It's an event or feeling or status change in the future. It's how someone's life is better after working with you.

Earlier we wrote about the better future that someone will experience if they work with you. That future transformation, who they'll become, what they'll experience. That future life is the benefit and that's what they're buying. Sometimes, that singular transformation is enough to sell a product. The future that you describe can be enough to convert someone into buying. However, we need to go deeper and be more emotive with our benefits, and that's where we turn each milestone into a benefit. The question we're asking is "So what?" So what if I appear on more podcasts? So what if I promote a sales webinar? So what if I pass that milestone? Remember WIIFM? What's In It For Me? That's the only radio station that your customers are tuned into. Whereas promotion on podcasts and blogs might make sense to you, don't take for granted that your customer knows why it matters. So what, they're asking? So what's in it for me?

You can download our Product Result Benefit Worksheet at sellyourservice.co.uk/fivefigurefunnels or grab a piece of paper and divide it into three columns. At the top of column one write Product, column two write Result and column three write Benefit. In the Product column write out the milestones that you're delivering to the customer. Nothing fancy, just the name of the milestone you've got in your product so far. For example, we'll choose milestone 2 from our example above, Create A Sales Webinar. In the Results column, write out all the measurable results that this milestone is working towards and/or achieves. These are more factual and numerical based outcomes. It's the first level of "So what?" So what if I create a sales webinar? What's in it for me? These results will usually be pretty easy to think of; there are only so many things that you'll improve and impact on in a business. An easy way to write out the results is to look at your steps under the milestone and ask what that step does for the business. What does it give to the customer? *Why* do we do this step? What result does it deliver to us?

For example:

Product	Result
Create a sales webinar	Gives us a repeatable, scalable piece of sales content that delivers a consistent sales message and works 24 hours a day. It also gives us authority and credibility with an audience by educating them before we make a pitch.
Use the language, desired result and desired problems to solve as the topic for a sales webinar	Gives us easy topic ideas and the framework for a webinar using language and problems that the customer already connects with. Typically increases lead capture/sign up conversion rates compared to webinars that don't include this.
Outline 3 methods for solving the problem or achieving the desired result	Demonstrates expertise and knowledge and proves that we can help the customer and we know what we're talking about.
Create a product or offer to sell on the webinar at the end of the call	Capitalises on webinar attendance and interest and provides us with income and sales. Increases revenue.
Explain a myth or misconception that prevents people from achieving those results or solving those problems	Overcomes a typical objection in the webinar attendees mind when they hear about the problem we can solve and allows us to show that it's not their fault if they've tried it before. Typically increases sales conversion rates compared to webinars that don't include this.
Include credibility and authority slides to explain who you are	Make it clear that you're the expert and that you can help them. Demonstrates knowledge and that you've done this before. Typically increases sales conversion rates compared to webinars that don't include this.
Make sure the content will be suitable for evergreen promotion	Gives us a repeatable, scalable piece of sales content that delivers a consistent sales message and works 24 hours a day. It also gives us authority and credibility with an audience by educating them before we make a pitch. Also means we don't have to change the webinar recording and redo it.

Figure 4: Product Result Table

In the above example, I've written out a series of results that each stage and milestone gives. You'll also notice a few things: For one, there are repetitions. That's absolutely fine, repetition is GOOD. In fact, as we get closer to benefits and write out more benefits and results for all our milestones and steps, we'll see that there are lots of overlaps and repeated benefits and results. That's how you get known for something. If you create 36 methods for converting email subscribers into customers, you're 36x more likely to be known for converting email subscribers into customers. You'll also notice that the results are what the product gives to us *now*. It's what the step, milestone or product delivers to our door.

Why do we make sure the content is suitable for evergreen promotion? So we can use it 24 hours a day at scale and so we don't have to redo it. If we asked a customer "Would you like a sales message that was delivered with 100% accuracy, at scale, 24 hours a day and you only have to do it once?" that would most likely be a "Yes". The result is something the customer understands. Lastly, we sometimes are affecting a numerical result or metric within businesses that are typically considered important. Leads, sales, subscribers, audience, revenue, profit, traffic etc. The more of these we can include, the better. This is the start of building an offer. We're starting to collect a list of results that we can deliver to the customer. We're also building a list of content ideas *hint*.

When we build a pitch deck or sales letter or when we're talking to a customer, we can start talking about results. Results are what matter and these make the sale. However, we need to go one step further. We need to look at the benefits. Benefits as we've mentioned before are the better future that the customer experiences after working with you. I think people overcomplicate benefits which is funny because I think people oversimplify them when they teach them. And perhaps it's because they're oversimplified that we overcompensate, by overcomplicating them.

We all think that when we try to discover and create benefits for our products, we try to get clever by telling people *why* this feature matters. I always remember being taught that electric windows had a benefit over manual crank windows on a car. Although I never really understood how anyone could create a benefit from such a menial feature. Almost every car has electric windows right? And those that don't have electric windows but still have manual windows are bought by people that don't care about electric windows. This is when my sales coach, by the name of Sean Mize, explained to me that you **don't sell the feature, you sell the buyer.** You look for areas of their life that will be better and perhaps more importantly, justified, when they buy that feature. For example, electric windows are the feature. The benefit is *not* "it makes the window easier to roll down when it's hot". That's what most people position as a benefit. They look at what the feature does. But as we'll see later, your job is to *sell futures, not features*. The benefit of the

76

electric window is the future that the customer experiences. The benefit is sold *to* the customer. For example "imagine sitting in your brand new car and feeling just how warm the weather is outside. You could switch on the AC, but the fresh air feels and sounds so much better. Can you remember what it was like when you were a teenager and you got your first car? The feeling of freedom? Rolling down the windows playing your favourite music as you drive somewhere *you* want to drive to? Electric windows aren't convenience, they're freedom. They're a sign that you're here to do what you want, when you want, listening to music that you want."

That might seem like a massive stretch but that message of the future and benefits is 100x stronger than the convenience of "Easier to roll down windows." Having said that, you could really lean into the convenience angle. For example, "You work hard. You drive to work and know that you're going to do everything you can today to make something happen. Your boss makes things difficult and management are constantly getting in your way. Your inbox is full of complaints, work-requests, spam and work-committee-forwards. It's a lot to deal with and it's not going to stop. You want to make sure that something *works*. That when you push that button, it's a smooth operation and responds immediately. It's a hot day, the office will be muggy and stuffy. Imagine sitting in your car waiting to enter the office knowing that you can guarantee that your car works perfectly, right down to the windows. You deserve things that work, you deserve to have a small convenience that makes your life just a little easier because everything else is getting tougher."

Overkill maybe? The reality is that unless you're this committed to your product you're going to struggle to sell anything, yet alone a marketing funnel. You have to imagine a bright, brilliant future that you customers want. It's about describing this beautiful future they could have and you are willing to make it happen for them. That's what selling marketing funnels is about. Heck, that's what *selling* is about. Microsoft doesn't sell Windows and Office. They sell productivity and 'Getting it done'. Jocko Willink doesn't sell books and podcasts. Jocko sells belief and strength. Most people are after a few basic things. We already have the necessities covered - food, water, shelter. Those are a given. Almost everything we sell now is intangible. It's stuff that as human beings we don't need but as people with personalities and thoughts and feelings, we do. We desire connection, a sense of contribution and status amongst our peers. We desire meaningful relationships and to create things. We desire freedom, power and respect. Is it just about sex? I don't think it's that simple. But at a base level, the more you can improve someone's idea of what *they* think it takes to attract a mate, you won't be far wrong. That's why some people buy sports cars, some people buy Botox and some people buy travel. Can marketing funnels increase attractiveness or the other intangible desires? They sure as hell can.

On your Product, Result, Benefit sheet I want you to look at the final column and start writing the benefits to the results. Why does someone care about those results? Why does it affect them? How is their life better? If you find you're repeating a lot of benefits for the results and products, that's good. We want to repeat and build up strong case studies for those benefits. In the benefits column I want you to write what *your* niche becomes, feels and experiences after working with you. After they achieve a particular result, how does that benefit their life? How is their future better and brighter? I've got some examples below, continuing from the table above.

Can you see that many of these benefits are emotive and internal or reflective? They're not things, they're events or experiences. They're statuses and feelings - things that can't be touched. Those benefits are what you're selling. And the better you understand your audience, the better your benefits will be. On that note, even a strong benefit won't help sell a great product if the customer doesn't want it. Even if they need it, they won't buy unless they want it. If your niche or customer doesn't want the future you're building, you can't sell it. A badly positioned benefit to an audience that does want it is 100x stronger than a well written and clear benefit to those that don't want it. Write out your benefits for each step and milestone. You'll have an arsenal of benefits to sell to your audience and it'll make the rest of your business much easier.

Product	Benefit
Create a sales webinar	In the future, after working with me, my customers feel complete confidence in their sales approach. They know that every customer is being given the same consistent sales pitch and that their product is being shown in the best possible light.
Use the language, desired result and desired problems to solve as the topic for a sales webinar	In the future, after achieving this step, my customers become the trusted advisor to their customers and audience. They're able to help more people than ever and they're paid above average fees for their expertise.
Outline 3 methods for solving the problem or achieving the desired result	Become the trusted advisor to their customers and audience. They're able to help more people than ever and they're paid above average fees for their expertise.
Create a product or offer to sell on the webinar at the end of the call	Become a powerful money making machine that sells to customers on automation and allows the director to focus on partnerships and strategy, rather than selling products to customers.
Explain a myth or misconception that prevents people from achieving those results or solving those problems	Transforms the business into a freethinking disruptor who doesn't compete with the usual market because they're going totally against the grain and positions themselves as a unique and valuable asset to their audience.
Include credibility and authority slides to explain who you are	Become the trusted advisor to their customers and audience. They're able to help more people than ever and they're paid above average fees for their expertise.
Make sure the content will be suitable for evergreen promotion	Start leaving work at 3pm, confident that all leads and prospects are being sold to while you take the rest of the day off. The less you work, the higher your income.

Figure 5: Product Benefit Table

Who benefits, who suffers?

It's not enough to just write out the benefits to your product. You need to connect at a deeper level with *who* benefits and *who* suffers if you do/don't make the sale. No matter how clear you are on your product, you still need to create enough enthusiasm to sell to people who aren't warm to you. 99% of the time, your clients aren't going to be immediately interested in buying from you. They might want the benefits, they might even want the product. You just haven't transferred enough enthusiasm to them for them to buy. Also, your motivation is going to wane. You can't 'be' 10/10 all the time and the rejection and silent marketplace isn't going to help that. You need to see a way to push past objections and push past your lack of motivation. Finally, connecting with *who* will help you connect with customers. Remember, in order to sell anything we have to serve an audience, and when you can't help but think of who benefits and suffers if you sell/quit, you'll become obliged to carry on and push forward.

Take a piece of paper and at the top, write 'Who Benefits?' This is going to be a list of everyone who will benefit if you make the sale. If you convert the customer, and the customer buys, who benefits from that decision? We're going to get really deep into it. I want you to start thinking wider and bigger than just yourself and the customer. For example, our product is an email marketing system for authors launching a course. If you make that sale, who benefits? We're going to write out a list of who benefits *and* how they benefit:

- The customer benefits because they now have a profitable product that sells well and makes them money
- You benefit because you're being fairly rewarded for your expertise
- Your customer's customers benefit because they now can learn a new skill, perhaps changing their life forever.
- Your bank manager is happy because they don't have to call you about unpaid bills
- Your customer's family benefit because they see how important this is to them and how happy it makes them
- Your chosen email platform account manager benefits, they just found a new customer too!

You want to go on and on and on? Looking at who benefits from the close, who benefits from the sale and how do they benefit? Why is this a good thing for them? You can list as many benefits as you want for each person too. For example, a product like this benefits the customer's family in multiple ways: they can afford to go on holiday; they'll see their Mum, Dad, Son, Daughter etc. succeed at something they care about. Your family benefits; the local economy benefits; staff and hires benefit. Go wide and big on who benefits as a result of your ability to sell this product. Imagine the butterfly effect of getting this project off the ground. Imagine how many lives you could affect through closing this deal? Even the smallest marketing funnel project could literally change lives. Think about how books, cheaper than a meal at McDonalds, have totally changed your life and the life of those around you. It's not arrogant or selfish to think something to be this big. If anything it's the opposite of that. You're not just thinking about yourself. You're thinking about the wider world and the impact you'll have on hundreds or even thousands of people. When you have this list, it'll keep you focused on moving forward and getting the work done - but we're still not done yet. We need to look at who suffers.

Who suffers if you don't complete the sale? Who suffers if you miss the mark and don't close? Again, a similar exercise. Grab a piece of paper and write 'Who Suffers?' at the top. Now we're going to write a list of people whose life is worse if we miss the sale. How is their life worse? Who suffers and why would they suffer if you didn't sell this product? Look beyond you and the customer; look at the people who you wrote about in your Who Benefits list. How is their life worse if they don't buy? Go wide, go big. What about suppliers? Local businesses? If you don't make the sale are you going to buy the locally made garden table you wanted? If you don't close the sale, would your customer's family be upset seeing how hard your potential customer is working, but without getting anywhere? Nothing is harder to watch than someone you love fail at something they love doing.

I know that, I've seen it happen. For a long time, my partner Olivia couldn't run. She loves running more than anything in the world and it was taken from her. We had a car crash and while I got off better than her, she lost more because it took years of rehab, therapy and failure before she could run at her previous standard again. I genuinely thank every single therapist and runner and specialist who sold her expensive and lengthy treatment to get her better. We travelled all over the world looking for help and those that could help, charged us for it and I will be forever grateful for their patience and commitment to Olivia to get her running again. And frankly, I'll always be disappointed in those that refused to close her. Refused to sell and treat her for one reason or another. The choice about whether the product can help someone or not, is not your choice. Who are you to decide to quit on someone when they need help? Is it because it's uncomfortable? Is it because you don't like asking for money? Can you imagine telling someone that they can't run again because you feel a bit weird asking for money? This 'suffering' angle is all about guilt. It's about putting your feelings and anxieties aside and giving you perspective. Understanding how other people suffer because of your decisions is how great progress is made.

Sticking with the medical angle. Imagine you're a doctor and you can see someone has broken their leg and it's bad. Really bad. It's a compound fracture which, not to dwell on it, means the bone has broken through the skin. Fractures like this can be life threatening. You as the doctor manage to get the injured person, who is now YOUR patient, to a hospital and you explain to them what needs to happen. You're going to have to set the bone which is very uncomfortable to say the least. Even with painkillers, it's pretty rough. Then we might need to operate on the bone and put some pins in before sewing you up and giving you more painkillers. You'll need a lot of rehab and rest and even after it's healed, you'll have to take it easy and get back to strength. Then, I want you to imagine that the patient says "No thanks" and tells you that they'll just leave it as it is. And if you don't think that happens, spend some time in a hospital. The number of refusals of help from staff for patients, is crazy high. People will often reject help for lots of different reasons.

As the doctor, do you simply accept the response and say "OK!" and go looking for another patient? Of course not. You'd be considered a monster if you did that. You'd be weak. You're clearly not in it for the right reasons. You know better than the patient. You know best. You are the expert. You push past the objections and nos. You know that their life will be much much worse in the long run for the sake of a few moments of pain. You even know that they'll thank you today if you get it over and done with. Does this mean that when we sell, we ignore the no? We want to know the reasons behind their decision and I'll leave it to your best judgement on whether to push through it or not. Do you think they should eat their vegetables or not? Who knows best? Will their life be worse if they never eat their vegetables? Do you think they should go to sleep, or stop eating junk food, or quit their job? Who suffers if you don't work and why is their life worse? Write out that list.

XYZ Statement

Most funnel builders will tell people "I run a marketing company" or "I build marketing funnels". And as I've mentioned before, that just doesn't interest people. We need to tell them how we help and who we help. Who we work with is more important than what we do. With that said, we have a simple process for writing out clearly and succinctly what our answer should be for when people ask "What do you do?" I call it an XYZ Statement and it looks like the below.

We work with X type of people, who have Y type of problem to achieve Z result.

This framework can be used to answer people when they ask what you do. It'll help them understand how you can help them, if at all, and if you're the right person to talk to. It's also the most powerful tool for rising above your competition. We've talked about how so many funnel businesses are middle of the road, and frankly, aren't that clear on what they do themselves. So, when we can clearly explain and articulate how we help people and who we work with, we're already separating ourselves from the average funnel business in the market. Another thing the XYZ gives us is clarity. When you have a solid XYZ Statement, it's easier to create content and products. It is easier to find customers and attract an audience, all because your statement guides what you should be helping people do. Let's look at some examples first and then dig into how to create a winning XYZ statement for yourself.

We work with female course creators who need
to keep more recurring membership clients in order
to grow their member base.

This example is pretty easy to understand and has a clear focus on what the business is doing to help that audience. What I love about statements like this is that even if you don't 100% match the XYZ, you still might be interested. For example, the process presumably of retaining members isn't exclusive to female course creators. So other types of businesses will ask "can you also help me?"

We motivate health result coaches to launch a
new product every year without wasting or losing
thousands of dollars to product development.

This example switches around the statement structure to XZY (characteristic, result, problem) but as you can see, still clearly defines who they work with and how that person can benefit. Notice that we also change the language slightly from 'help' or 'work with' to a more dynamic adjective. Help as a word is overused and there are so many more interesting and definitive words to use. Motivate, inspire, create, build, define, discover, construct, encourage, incentivise. Look at your core values and beliefs and understand which behaviour you think is important for people to improve or unlock.

We partner with individuals with over 1m
YouTube subscribers who help their audience
discover the best technology deals to save money
and build products that they own so they can create
security within their business and brand.

A longer XYZ but still following the structure of X person, Y problem and Z result. The definition is much longer on this which is a positive. I bet you could think of 10 blog post ideas right now to help someone in that situation. Many online influencers have a brand but no products. They technically don't even have distribution as YouTube, Facebook and Instagram have notorious changes in their policies and algorithms that can totally destroy a process which was working for people with large followings. A funnel builder could easily look at a way of converting that current audience into an email list (owned distribution) and help the influencer build a product or at least product partnership that creates a more stable business. As funnel builders, it's critical that we create an offer which is clearly about the customer. We get far too wrapped up in trying to explain the benefits of the product, or worse, educating them on the features (which is massively overrated). Instead, if you can explain the benefits the customer will experience in their life compared to who they are, and a defining characteristic that they recognise, like overcoming a problem they're experiencing, they are more likely to become interested. Also, you're more likely to have a clear idea on how to create content for your business as well as attract a specific niche and position yourself as an apex marketer.

How to sell a squeeze page

I wanted to include an example of a squeeze page product or offer that you could sell to your customers. I want to highlight that even a simple 3 page funnel like a squeeze funnel can provide massive results to your clients and how you can sell a product to your audience without telling them what it is. Sell futures, not features. Maybe you love the idea of building squeeze pages for customers but you don't really know how to sell them. Maybe you just like the idea of selling them to customers but you think "How do I actually convince someone to buy this from me?" It might be that you've never really thought that squeeze pages were a viable product option for you to be able to sell, but squeeze pages provide massive benefits to businesses if you can sell them and set them up correctly. I think we undervalue squeeze pages because they're so easy to set up. The page builders like Beaver Builder and Elementor and Divi have all of these templates built into their products and we think because it's easy to build, it can't be valuable and therefore I can't sell one.

I'm here to tell you that if you wanted to, you could sell a squeeze page package for $10,000 or £25,000. It's not about what you deliver. It's the results you get for the customer and the future that you're delivering to them. If you believe that customers won't buy squeeze pages from you, you are sorely mistaken. Customers absolutely will buy squeeze pages from you if you position them correctly. It really is more than just one page. First of all, you're physically not just delivering a squeeze page. I talk later about the kinds of the products you need to package together in order to sell squeeze pages, but it's more than just a web page. It could be a 24 hour lead generation process. For them, it could be a way for them to measure their SEO and analytics more effectively; it could be a way of reducing their cost per advertising or their cost per acquisition; it could be a way of increasing their conversion rates. The squeeze page could be a way for them to generate a whole load of qualified leads for their business; it could be a way for you to be able to generate proposals and quotes for a customer by having their customers fill out a report or a form.

You're not just selling a page, what you're giving people is a massive amount of control over the types of customers that reach their business. What you're doing is creating a filter that attracts the right type of customer and turns away the wrong type of customer. That's what the squeeze page does. At its core, this is about scalable lead generation and that's really what I want you to have in the back of your mind. Squeeze pages are about helping businesses generate leads at scale. It's about helping them generate more leads than they've ever done before and done well and at scale, but without necessarily having more time invested in it.

Here's the package that I would put together. First of all, I would create the squeeze page itself, you might even want to create two slight variations so they can split test it because customers love that. And that could just be a headline or one column or two columns. You also want to give them a thank you page. The very basic high level lead generation funnel we should build is where people sign up, but they're not taken to the product straight away, or the PDF of the download or the lead magnet. A lot of people offer a free cheat sheet in exchange for typing in an email address. Then they'll redirect the new lead to that PDF. That's not what we're going to do; we're going to take them to a *thank you page* and on that thank you page we're going to have a video sales letter. The video sales letter (VSL) can upsell them to the first product they can buy. And it might BE A £9 or £19 product or £2,000 product. You're also going to confirm the action the lead took and acknowledge the action they took and tell them that on the thank you page.

"Thanks so much for giving us your email address. We've sent your download and your cheat sheet to the email address you gave us. If you want to change it, click here."

In the email that is sent to them you have the delivery page with the content. You're going to deliver those three things to a squeeze funnel. The squeeze page, the thank you page and the delivery page. A thank you page allows you to measure conversions and allows you to confirm that people have signed up. It's also a perfect opportunity to upsell products to people. The delivery page can have an upsell video. What this does is first of all eliminate spam email addresses so you don't get fakeemail@gmail.com. You're saying "If you want this free report or lead magnet, you've got to give us your real email address."

The squeeze funnel product then becomes the process of converting and capturing leads 24 hours a day, being able to completely accurately measure the conversion rate between the page and potentially reducing the cost per acquisition on the initial traffic page. So, if you're using remarketing or even cold traffic through ads to drive people to these squeeze pages, that's where you're going to be able to start measuring your conversions is on the thank you page. First of all, lower cost of acquisition, lower cost per click, lower advertising costs, increased insight on the conversion rates that you've got, and you're capturing and converting leads 24 hours a day. We're also going to increase the quality of the type of lead and customer that does reach your customer because if someone downloads a cheat sheet on 'the best headphones to use while playing video games', you know that they both play video games and they're in the market for new headphones. They are giving you market indicators that they are in the market for a product. This is also a really fast way for a business to be able to build a brand that's known for a result.

For example, I give away training on how to sell marketing funnels. And wouldn't you know that by doing that 24 hours a day I become known for helping people sell marketing funnels. The lead magnets and the capture pages and the squeeze pages that you're selling is bigger than just a squeeze page to capture email addresses and build an email list, although that's a big part of it. You're helping them build a brand. You're helping to put out a result that people will begin to expect the same level of service from. It's about delivering on those expectations through multiple different channels. And that's what you're delivering with a squeeze page

Squeeze funnels have a tendency to shorten the sales cycle as well. Whereas we used to get leads the old fashioned way, where people just give you their email address, almost instantaneously we've seen conversions go from 50 days or 30 days to 0 days or one day because we have the upsell page immediately on the thank you page. Also, there's a self liquidating offer where if it costs you £1 to get a lead conversion and you know that you have 10 leads, equalling £10. And then 1/10 people buys a £10 product, that £10 product has paid for all of those lead conversions.

You've got all of those leads for free. If you're smart you can start helping your customers generate leads for free. If you can help your customers generate leads for free you will never be short on customers. And this is all the result of a basic squeeze page package for your customers. Can you see now how a squeeze page package can be worth £25,000? You say to the customer "We're going to run through this process. We're going to do a bunch of tests with all the traffic that you currently drive. What if we could reduce your advertising costs to zero?" That's a seriously compelling package.

Summary

- What you're ultimately selling is transformation. Customers are buying a better future version of themselves
- All your products and services should be helping them transform into something they want to be
- Your price points should reflect how quickly you can get them there depending on how much they invest
- Sell Futures, Not Features

AUTHORITY

It breaks my heart to see so many talented, smart and dedicated funnel builders fail to be recognised for the value they can add to people's lives. Every single person reading this book could comfortably become a leading expert in a field and reap the rewards that follow such expertise. In this chapter we're going to build you into an authority in a specific area and show you what happens when you are an authority.

You don't need a portfolio

How are you going to sell a squeeze page product to authors, if you've never *built* a squeeze page just for authors before? Have you ever had a prospect get close to buying, but then at the last minute ask you "Have you got an example of any work you've done before?" The portfolio is the necessary evil of the digital creative. Showing previous work seems like such a critical and important part of the process that it seems bizarre or even dangerous for me to suggest that you don't need a portfolio at all.

When you have decided your niche and decided the type of offer you want to bring to the market, the first thing your customers will want to see is a portfolio. They'll want to see previous work right? But it's a Catch 22, you can't show people work you haven't done and you can't get the work without a portfolio. So where do you start? Most business experts and instructors will tell you to do free work until you build up a portfolio. Sounds sensible right? It's all about that hustle and grind! How often have you heard someone say "I'm doing this cheaply because I want to build up my portfolio"? If you're starting a brand new enterprise or focusing on a new niche and you know that you're selling them for at least £10,000, then how does *free* really work for you? It's a lot of work for the sake of a portfolio.

Another idea I see floating around is to do some 'fake' projects and list them under your portfolio. Build a few funnels for fake businesses and claim them on your portfolio. Not a terrible idea, but again, it's missing the point.

Firstly, most people who work on their portfolio or insist on building fake projects are procrastinating. They're avoiding the fact that they are going to have to go out there and sell. Busy work through doing low paid, low value work or even free work, is a very good way of avoiding getting on the phone, meeting people at networking events and pitching them or selling to them. Later on in this book I'm going to give you my exact process for finding your first customer AND you do not/will not need a portfolio.

Secondly, I'll gladly do free work for someone even if they don't ask me to, if I think it's a good way to land a larger customer. In the early days, I'd build a basic 3 page funnel for a business and literally *give* it to them as a way to get my foot in the door. The difference is that I chose the business and had a better idea that they could afford my larger packages. If someone asks *you* to work for free or low pay, or if you 'sell' it to them cheaply, they'll never have more money to spend in the long term. Thirdly and finally, the reason customers want a portfolio is NOT to see other examples of your work. They might say that and they might even think that, but the reason people ask for portfolios is because they don't trust you.

Etiquette dictates that we don't outwardly say "I don't trust you and/or the product", so they dance around the subject. "Have you got examples of previous work? Can we see your portfolio? Have you done this kind of project before?" The reason they're asking these questions is because they have an **objection**. An objection is the reason someone doesn't buy. They might say it's because of the price, or they want to see a portfolio or they need time to think about it. But really deep down, it's because they don't trust you or the solution.

The reason that you don't need a portfolio is because there are other faster, easier and more effective ways to grow your trust with someone. A portfolio is one of the ways we can demonstrate that we know what we're doing. It's a way of building trust with the customer, but it's not the *only* way. This is why we create Authority through content.

CS Case Study - Landing the deal with zero experience

CS is a customer of ours from when we ran an agency. At the time (they've since grown) they were a £500,000+ turnover business that consults businesses on strategic thinking. Global offices, celebrity endorsers, six figure projects. They were the perfect customer.

We landed our first five figure deal with CS, without a portfolio or examples of previous work. In fact, they never even asked to see a portfolio because we had something better. We had a long form, high quality piece of killer content (over 10,000 words) that we sent to them and talked them through. Following the lead generation process that I'll share with you later, we wanted to build membership sites for businesses that consulted their customers who wanted to scale their process. Building online educational material for their business is a fantastic way to scale and reach new customers and we had the exact process to do that.

We asked around if anyone in our network knew of "consultancy businesses that were looking to scale their program delivery through online courses" and a mutual friend put me in touch with N. N. who is the founder and CEO of CS. I asked if I could come in and show him how we can help them scale their delivery. Before going in, I sent him my long form piece of content which was a 10,000 word guide on 'How membership businesses can grow their email lists'. It had worksheets, free downloads, content upgrades and images; it was basically a short book. This piece of content coupled with my workshop and discovery process lead us to land a deal in a couple of weeks and get paid. No portfolio, no objections.

Only an expert could write 10,000 words

"But Mike, I've never *built* this particular funnel before…".

Then go ahead and build one. Build a version of your product, similar to how we mentioned the fake projects above and document that process. If you really feel you need the practice, then do it first as a dry run. Hell, do it for your own business first. In truth, you shouldn't need to build the entire funnel even when you do land customers because your process isn't how to build anything, it's how to transform the customer's life. And experts like you need to be experts in transformation.

At a high level, the idea is that we create enough content to position you as an authority. Let's say I had a blog post that was over 10,000 words long talking about how to sell a marketing funnel to a customer. What if I had a blog post on *just* talking about how to PRICE a marketing funnel? Does that amount of copy and content suggest that I really know what I'm talking about when it comes to the hyper-specific topic of pricing a marketing funnel?

Expert status isn't something given to you, it's something you build. There's no diploma or award ceremony that bestows the title of expert status. Lots of people feel they need to be an expert before they write the book. It's as if the International Board Of Expert Certification hands you the title of expert because of your work in the field, and *then* you're asked to write the book. It's the other way around. The more content you create around a topic, the more you are seen as the expert. It has to be enough to demonstrate that you could talk for hours on it, and it has to be specific enough to show that you're the expert in that field.

I'm not considered the worlds #1 sales coach for funnel builders just because I've sold a lot of funnels. In fact, I'd argue that I definitely have not. But, I have published more content and longer pieces on *just* selling marketing funnels than anyone else. That's my exercise for building trust with readers and customers. You're literally reading a book called "Five Figure Funnels: How to sell marketing funnels for over £25,000". That's why I can say "I wrote the book on it."

The idea is that only two types of people write over 10,000 words on a subject. An expert or a crazy person. Assuming you're not crazy, the consensus will be that you're an expert because surely only an expert would have this much to say about a subject! This long form, high quality killer content will *replace* the need for a portfolio.

Should you write a book? Yes, absolutely. You absolutely should write a book with over 40,000 words in it and run it through print on demand. If you want the *ultimate* portfolio, then write and self publish a book. Not just for the kudos but because surely only an expert would write this much on one topic. Lot's of businesses get caught up in the idea of 'branding' and building a brand. They'll get logos and colour schemes done, brand assets and palettes and brand guidelines. If you want to build a brand, which is to say, if you want to become so well known for something that your name is synonymous with a topic, then you need to publish content. And it all starts with the 10,000 killer blog post or Authority Content.

You're already an expert

Our society values experts and expert opinion. We place trust in those who seemingly know better and look to them for guidance. When it comes to your initial niche and topic, it's easy to start doubting your expert status and whether you truly have anything to offer. I argue that you absolutely are an expert and you know more than you think.

Firstly, it's easy to think about all the topics and knowledge you have and believe that you aren't teaching things people don't already know. Let's say that your niche is authors looking to launch a second book and build a course with it. You might not own a course software or SaaS business; you're not an author (yet); you see tons of other experts teaching about course design and course websites, membership funnels etc.; you're exposed to the vast array of potential knowledge out there and you realise how much you don't know. It's a classic phenomenon often labeled as 'imposter syndrome'.

Imposter syndrome is the lack of belief in your skills compared to those around you, certain that if you draw attention to yourself you'll be called out and labelled a fraud. For example, you could be working with a customer and halfway through the meeting they stop, look at you and say "You don't know what you're talking about do you?" After all, there are so many experts out there with books, courses, shows, interviews and blogs that you couldn't possibly know as much as them. Therefore, why even label yourself as an expert in that field when you know for a fact, almost everything you teach will be a derivative of something you learned from them? Eventually, the world finds out that you've been fraudulently misleading people and claiming other people's knowledge as your own. You are extradited from civilisation and banished to the land of wind and ghosts. Imagine how your mother will feel.

That is imposter syndrome talking. It's a defence mechanism your brain puts in place that demonstrates your knowledge of your *lack* of knowledge. You know how much you don't know. It's why teenagers can't be taught or shown how *wrong* they are. Their naivety stems from a lack of experience and their cocksure attitude just demonstrates how little they have truly experienced. They have no idea how big the world really is and can't compare their life experience to a larger context. They *don't* know what they don't know. I'm being overly harsh on teenagers, when really I mean adolescents, of which we can all be during stages of our lives or with certain activities. Driving for example, we all think we're experts in this, but *someone* must be crashing cars. An adolescent attitude to life is the opposite of imposter syndrome. Imposter syndrome is useful to an extent because it shows that you're not a sociopath. When you reach a certain level of experience and understanding, you break past the beginner barriers and see just how much is out there. To most people for example, they'll say they know how a toilet works. If you ask people to rank themselves on how much they know about how a toilet works, they'll rank themselves quite highly. That is until you ask them to explain how a toilet works in as much detail as possible. All of a sudden they realise they're below even an amateur status.

So how can we combat imposter syndrome? I've stated that you're already an expert. How can you believe that? It's very simple. One a scale of 1 - 7, where would you rank yourself compared to everyone else in the world, on your chosen subject? 1 being total newbie, 7 being world's #1 expert. Be honest, don't think about it too much. If you think you're a 2, put 2. If you think you're a 5 or 6, put that down.

Ask other people too, where they rank themselves and then where they rank you. *Hint:* the goal is NOT to get the highest number possible, this is an exercise in context. After you've got a good idea of your X/7 score, write it down and draw a triangle or pyramid (like an upside down funnel) with the wide base at the bottom and the top being the point. Along the side of the triangle starting with the number 1 at the bottom, write the numbers 1 to 7 along the side going up the triangle. So 1 is the bottom and 7 is the point at the top. It'll look something like the below.

Figure 6: Expert Ranking Pyramid

Circle where you rank yourself and draw a line horizontally, across the triangle. Everyone below that line could benefit from talking to you. Everyone above that line has something to offer you. Here's where this gets interesting. Let's say that you rank yourself a 3/7. So you draw a line across the 3 and think "Look how many people know more than me" and that's the wrong angle. That's the glass half empty, man.

Instead, let's look <u>under</u> the line. You are valuable to everyone who is a 1/7, which by the way is the largest part of the market, everyone who is a 2/7 and probably most people who are 3/7. You are considered an expert by the largest part of the market because the largest part is the foundation or beginner market. And to them, you might as well be a sorcerer or enchantress - you're doing pure magic.

Now, write a few names of people at the very top of the pyramid who you consider to be 7/7 experts. Who are the kings and queens of your industry? For me, Ryan Deiss, Mike Michalowicz and Jim Rohn are up there.

Write out *why* they're in the top position. Do they have books, podcasts, interviews, blog posts, websites, products, speaking gigs? Write out everything that makes them an expert. What exactly is stopping you from being as big an expert as them? Notice that all the characteristics that make an expert are things that you could also do. There's nothing preventing you from doing the same work as them to get to that position. Finally, is there that much of a gap between you and the top? After seeing what they do, are you really closer to a 4/7 or a 5/7?

You're already an expert, you're just not <u>positioned</u> as one. You've got it all locked away in your head and you need to get it out. No, at the moment you're not commanding the fees and coverage that the big guys are, but you will get there, they've just been doing it longer.

How to write 10,000 words

This is the scary bit. How do you now sit down and type out 10,000 words of content? It seems overwhelming because either a) you've never written that much before or b) you don't think you're a strong writer.

Admittedly, like most skills, the more you do this the easier it gets. Your first 10,000 words will be harder than your next 10,000 words. It's worth talking about a book too, which you should begin to think about. Your book will be 40,000 - 70,000 words and is the next level of authority content. But for now, let's stick with the 10,000 word post. The good news is that you've already written most of it, you just need to get it out of your head onto the screen.

There are dozens of books on writing, how to write, writing blog posts and writing hacks. However, I believe that no amount of reading will ever write 10,000 words. The only thing that will write 10,000 words is sitting down and typing 10,000 words. But there are frameworks that make it easier and faster to get your ideas on paper. So firstly, let's go over some high level principles to remember when starting to write:

1. Do not edit as you write. You're **writing** a blog post, not *editing* a blog post. Write, get your ideas out and spellcheck/edit later. Saying you're a perfectionist is procrastinating and won't do you any good.

2. It might take 10 or 20 minutes to get into the flow. The first 10 words are harder than the first 100 which are harder than the first 1000. Stick with it and write until you're done (either time or word count)

3. Writing is not a scrum tactic. Doing 5000 words in one go and leaving it for a few days will not help you. You're better off giving yourself 45 minutes a day to write. If you get into the zone and continue past that time, great, then continue. But don't have massive numbers written less frequently.

4. Stick to the goal. Either decide that you will write for 45 minutes a day or 1000 words a day. Sit down, lock the door, turn off your

phone and use the loo before you start! Move your fingers over the keyboard and type nonsense until you're used to typing and then just type. Allow a stream of consciousness to fall onto the page. We can edit later.

5. 10,000 words can easily be written in a week if you're focused. Giving yourself time each day will absolutely get those words out. In fact, most of the time you'll end up going over the word count, which is fine.

Now we need a structure to our blog post in order to get the writing down as fast and efficiently as possible. Bearing in mind you already have the outline written up, it's the milestones question from chapter 3. What milestones do customers need? Our blog post will be another product in our product menagerie. Similar to our product offer, our blog post will help people transform, when they've read it. The price will be free other than the time it takes to read it, but the goal of the 10,000 word blog post will be to help someone transform from where they are now to where they want to be. Overall, our blog post is designed to position us as an expert who has a written process for helping people. We're going to tell them what steps they need to take and explain the details of each step.

Will they need more than a blog post to totally transform their lives? Of course, but does this 10,000 word post demonstrate that you're willing to document and commit to a process that works? Absolutely. The blog post framework we'll be using is the below.

Headline

What will sell the blog post to the reader? What's their massive WANT and what pain do they want to solve? Ultimately, what is the transformation they're going on and what do they want to become or see in the future? Keep headlines short and specific. Write them last, after you've written the post.

Promise

Outline the promise you can make to the reader. Explain to them absolutely everything you're going to cover and the big takeaway they'll have when they finish reading the post.

The introduction to your content should outline the promise you intend to deliver. Why should anyone read, watch or listen to your content? How will they be transformed as a result? Ultimately, what is the end result you're promising if they read this post? You might want to write this part last.

E.g. In this article you will learn how to increase the conversion rate on your website in three simple steps.

Spend about 100 words talking through the final result that someone will achieve if they read and implement your system and advice.

Problem

What's the biggest problem your reader is facing? We can view this in two ways: Pain points or roadblocks.

A pain point is a problem the reader wants to solve. They're aware of it and they want it to go away. Usually, it's the opposite to the result you're promising in the section above.

- Growing debts
- Low sales volumes
- Sharp pain in the knee when running

Pain points are problems that they're looking to you to solve. If you can demonstrate how to eliminate a pain and remove a problem from a reader's life, they'll be eternally grateful.

A roadblock is something that prevents the reader from achieving their goals or fixing a problem. For example, in your 'promise' opening, you might have mentioned that you promise to fix the sharp pain in their knee. You *could* reiterate the problem in the problem section, but it might be better to use a roadblock based problem.

Or, if you've promised to help them achieve a goal, you might want to demonstrate your knowledge of the process by explaining the roadblock preventing those results.

- Want to buy a house - roadblock is getting a deposit together
- Increase Google search traffic - no idea how to increase rankings
- Want to sell products online - no audience to sell to

Do the best job you can expanding on the problem and try to do at least 500 words on the problem and what it feels like to the user to have that problem. Talk about the consequences if they don't fix the problem. The problem section will be around 1000 words.

Myth

What's a common misconception solving this problem or achieving this goal? What's something that they've already tried to do or something that other people do that doesn't work and fails? What's the truth to this? This is a place for you to demonstrate why you're different. You can spend around 500 - 1000 words talking about myths and misconceptions.

Changing

Explain what's changing, both threats and opportunities, to them and their marketplace. Focus on what happens if they don't take action now. What could happen if they do take action now?

Use the prompts of technology, and society to frame the consequences of what is changing in their marketplace. You can be both positive with opportunities and negative with consequences.

- Technological
- Economic
- Sociological

Spend about 1000 words talking about what's changing in the world.

Knife twist

Finish the sentence "... and to top it all off..."

This is where we really dig the knife in and drive home the big problem that they're facing and explore another symptom or pain point they're experiencing.

This only needs to be short, around 100 words.

Solution

Outline the solution and tell them what you're going to explain to them. Think of 3 to 7 learning points and opportunities or exercises to guide them through the process. The 3 - 7 learning points are going to be the 3 - 7 steps in your product process. If you have a process name, like we have FUNNELS or The Six A's, then introduce the name of the process.

You only need to spend 100 words introducing the solution.

3 - 7 points

Think about using an exercise or worksheet or cheat sheet for each step and offer it for free and without an optin gate. Talk people through each point and repeat the same 'problem, promise, myth, changing' outline above for each learning point tour through the problem and the solution to the learning point how to solve it and also how to go through the worksheet. My advice would be to bullet point this part first. Write out the 3 to 7 steps in your process, and flesh out each learning point. Treat each point like its own mini blog post and use the same promise problem myth structure from above per learning point. Give yourself the opportunity to talk or write through the entire point.

It really is as easy as talking someone else through what they should do during that part of the process. For example, let's say you have a three step process to helping people convert blog traffic into email subscribers. And you call it the ABC process. Automate, Blog, Capture. Use the individual steps within each milestone from the previous chapter and you'll come up with plenty of content for your blog post. Give yourself the time to write and the space to write it and eventually you'll come up with an extremely useful and powerful longform piece of content. This is where the bulk of your work will be. It probably needs to be between 6000 and 7000 words.

Summary

Wrap up the conclusion by answering an objection. Answer the question "What if…?" By this point, the reader has usually got an objection in their mind, like "It sounds like hard work." or "I don't know where to get this tool." Answer the objection and turn it, treating it like a FAQ. Go over your favourite point and talk about why your favourite part of the entire process. Then ask them for their feedback in the comments section below. The summary will need to be around 500 words long.

Conversion copy

Finally, talk about the ultimate lead magnet or content upgrade you're offering and work hard at the conversion copy to help someone understand that they can get these results even faster if they download your worksheets or content upgrade.

How do I write so much content?

One of the most common questions I'm asked is "How do I write so much content?" This is interesting to me as I don't believe I do write as much content as it seems. And if I could, I would write more than I am doing now! The only way I know how to write a book is to sit down and write part of that book every single day.

Rather than thinking about how much content you have to write, instead think about setting up a regular time and giving yourself a routine to write with. Whether you like it or not, your first attempt at a blog post won't be perfect. But the goal is in writing - the blog post first and then editing it later.

I don't believe writer's block exists. I believe anyone suffering from writer's block is either out of practice or not using a framework/template. If I ever struggle to write a YouTube script, a chapter of a book or a blog post it's usually because I'm not using a template to get my ideas out and start the ball rolling. Much like going to the gym, the hardest part is putting on your trainers. If you use that structure above and flesh out the solution/learning points first, then go back and answer the other questions such as promise, problem and myth, you'll have an easier time drawing that content out of you.

Finally, it's worth noting that I'm only able to write as much content as I do now, and at a relatively consistently high level, because I have done it badly for so long. My first few blog posts were unfocused and lacked themes and identity. It was only through consistently writing that I managed to find my own voice, writing style and had the practice to be able to write consistently. I also use dictation and transcription software such as Dragon Dictate, Rev and Otter.ai. If I have a spare hour I'll talk into a microphone on my laptop, PC or phone and send it off to be transcribed. Or, I will use dictation software to write out my content quickly and effectively. Be warned, dictation is in itself its own skill. In some respects it is harder than typing, as you have to speak in a manner which is unusual and very different to speech. But this is less a case of becoming a typist and more getting your ideas on paper to demonstrate how valuable you are to the world.

Aren't I giving everything away?

If you're writing up everything for free, it's reasonable to wonder what will now happen, now that you're giving everything away for free. This one of the most common objections to writing a book, blog post or doing regular video or podcast content - the fear that when you write up content for free, you're giving everything away. Surely if you give everything away then people won't need you? If you don't have this fear and you're comfortable knowing why it's so important to create content and publish it, feel free to skip this section. However, if you are still unsure on the value of writing and giving away content, please read on.

There's a few different ways to approach this problem, so I'm going to outline all my arguments for why you should write and create content. If you want to start selling marketing funnels for five figures (the goal of this book), content is going to help you sell your marketing funnel services for at least £25,000 plus.

1. Famous chefs have cookbooks

Gordon Ramsay, Nigella Lawson, Jamie Oliver, Martha Stewart. The list goes on of famous TV chefs who have mountains of books. And in most cases their books are designed to promote them as a chef. No one ever buys a cookbook and then thinks "Well now I don't need to go eat at one of their restaurants". Their cook books giveaway mountains of recipes and knowledge for a fraction of the price of eating at one of the restaurants. Even chefs that don't have restaurants, still produce cooking books because it's the best way of raising the profile of the author.

If you want people to pay £50+ £100+ per person at a restaurant, you have to prove that your food is worth this and you know what you're talking about. If anything, writing cookbooks for chefs increases the likelihood that someone would go to one of their restaurants, or purchase one of their ready meals, cookery programmes or cooking courses.

2. Humans aren't that clever

If you've read my blog, watched my YouTube videos and listened to my podcast, you probably wouldn't need to buy this book. If you read this book and implement absolutely everything to the letter you probably don't need any of my courses.

However, at the age of a child and going to school when our brains are designed to absorb knowledge at a faster rate than any other time in our life, we still have to be taught things multiple times in multiple different ways. The cold reality is that human beings just aren't clever enough to be able to absorb teaching and education from one source and <u>apply</u> it immediately to their life without some kind of repetition.

There may be ideas, concepts and phrases that people connect with and get clarity from. For example my phrase "Sell futures not features" is probably my most commented on and shared quote but it doesn't completely eliminate the need for any further sales training or education. If anything, what explaining a process does and writing content does is demonstrate just how much depth and complexity there is even to relatively simple processes. When you begin to explain the entire process to potential customers, they won't think "Great! Now I don't have to pay someone to do this", instead they'll realise how much work is involved and how little they know. And if they want help with it, and if they want the results faster and with less work from themselves, they'll need to hire someone to do it with them.

Anyone who reads your content and decides to do it for themselves, evidently isn't in the right stage to buy from you. You're not removing potential customers, you're eliminating people who aren't customers and never will be.

3. People want more of you

When you begin to publish content, a very bizarre phenomena happens. People will begin to get to know you and you'll get to know your readers. What's interesting though is that if someone learns something from you and you have helped them, they are now more likely to want to consume the rest of your content or to work with you. Human beings are social animals. And our ability to gossip and share information with one another was a massive survival tactic hundreds of thousands of years ago. We trust people who educate us.

So when you begin to educate and help your readers, they'll assume you can help them further and will want to start reading more of your content. It's more the rule than the exception that people desire to work with someone purely because they have read their content, not in spite of it. We admire people who write up processes, publish work and have something to say. We admire people who have got so many ideas and thoughts that they give some of them, if not most of them, away for free. If you give people a taste of working with you they want more of you.

4. If you've only got one idea, you don't deserve more customers

This is perhaps a slightly harsher truth, but one that I find really drives the point home. If you're afraid of writing up your process and sharing it with people for free, in case they steal it, it might be a sign that you don't have any other ideas. Marketing agencies are typically very closed off and insular. It's an entire economy and marketplace based around fear and lack of information. I remember when I first moved to the South-West of England, no way in hell would anyone in the website or marketing space ever write anything for free because they were terrified of people stealing their ideas.

"Surely if I write up this information my competition will steal it?" This is an interesting thought because where did you acquire it from in the first place? It can't have been pure isolated inspiration; you must have learned some of it from somewhere. And when I probed a little further about what their 'ideas' were, turns out they actually didn't have any ideas at all. For all their fear and resistance to writing and giving away free content, it turns out that they didn't have anything to say. If you're terrified about writing something for free and giving it away, is it possible it's because you don't have any ideas or anything to say in the first place?

I would hope that by reading this book I've demonstrated to you that that's not true and you have plenty of ideas and lots to say. But there comes a point where you will be giving away so much in your content and if you go further with books and video, you won't be able to keep up with the amount of new ideas you create.

In my second book Universe Fuel, I talk about how if you want more of something, help other people get that thing. If you want more ideas, help other people discover their ideas and give more of your ideas away. You'll be rewarded in turn with far more in abundance than you could ever possibly use. Artists who have remained consistently high in music charts and are now seen as legends have given away their songs for fractions of the cost it takes to think of the ideas, go through the experiences, write up the lyrics and music and produce the songs. Some artists have now even resorted to giving music away for free because they know that concert sales and merchandise are where the majority of their income lie. By giving away more of their ideas and concepts, they are in fact rewarded with an abundance of ideas in the future.

5. It proves you've got a process

Finally and perhaps the most important aspect of writing up anything, is that it shows you have a process. If you're looking for a differentiator or proof that you know you're doing, write up the process for doing it. I wouldn't approach some random person asking them if they had a cake recipe or if they knew how to edit a film. I've got no evidence that that person even works with food or video. However, if I search for someone who can teach me that because they've documented and published something, it proves they got a process. And if they've got a process, it means they've done it before and they're a good person to learn from.

Personally, I don't believe that education is the most powerful sales method. I think a lot of people go the wrong way and educate their customers to go elsewhere. However, as with most things there is a balance, and you must have a documented written process in order to demonstrate your knowledge and expertise. I'm becoming very tired of marketing professionals who tell me that they are experts and they have 20 years experience, but when I ask them how much work they have published or how much they have shared with the community they'll gladly reply "None". "People should pay me if they want to learn from me". Maybe that used to be the case mate, but we're in the 2020s now and that's not how the economy works. In fact, it hasn't worked like that for around a hundred years. It's a complete false economy that people should exclusively pay you, to benefit from your knowledge.

Successful and fast-growing businesses know that they have to give away a lot of value upfront in order to charge big bucks on the backend. There is an absolute direct proportion between the amount of value given upfront and the price tag you attach at the end. The same consultants who would proudly tell me that someone has to pay them to work with them, charge maybe ⅕th of what I would charge as a day rate. I have far more content out there. It's not a coincidence, that's just how a free market capitalist economy works.

Summary

- Experts have content. The expert status follows the content, not the other way around
- Customers want proof that you're the right person for the job and the easiest way to do that is with published documented content
- You're already an expert, you just need content to prove it
- Authority is completely free to build and can yield infinite results

ATTENTION

In this chapter we're going out to market and we're going to generate some leads, referrals and attention to both you and your business. If being the focus of attention makes your feel sick, then I've got good news. The real focus we'll be drawing attention to is the customer and their problems. We're going to be the spotlight, not in the spotlight.

Generate referrals

We now need to generate attention and interest in the marketplace in order to validate our ideas; start generating some income and some work. When you first start, your marketing funnel business is going to be very tempting to focus on building a new website - doing things like a logo; brand colours; domain name and social profiles. Most businesses believe that doing these kinds of activities is what results in new customers and sales.

In truth, most of these activities are just a form of procrastination: even if you build a brand-new website and choose a perfect logo that is both timeless and modern; even if you choose a fantastic domain name and business name that is clever and authoritative, it's still going to require you to generate sales for your business. Most business owners fall into the trap of ABS. Anything But Sales.

Even if you did have a website and we can prove this is true, so many businesses still rely on referrals. I personally know of many marketing agencies that have a great website and beautiful looking logos, design and brand, but still generate the majority of their work through referrals. While I believe referrals are an absolutely critical part of any business, it's their time and place in the sales and marketing process that makes a difference. Generating greenfield leads (greenfield meaning brand new to you and your wider social circle) is extremely important and a website. content and advertising will help you with that. So, referrals are extremely important but you must also be looking to the market for greenfield leads.

I understand this can seem confusing: I seem to be telling you to do both activities or neither activity. The distinction is WHEN you do these activities. When starting out as a brand-new business, now that you have your killer blog content, your job is to go to market and generate referrals. We've already talked about how your job is not to sell marketing funnels. You don't even build marketing funnels. Your job is to help your niche solve a particular problem and that's what you will be going to market with, in order to try and sell.

The problem with creating a website and investing heavily in the brand and marketing and advertising, is that you still end up in the same place as if you didn't do it. You won't generate sales just from having a beautiful website. The fastest way for you to start getting some work is to reach out to your network and have a conversation with them. It's likely that you know between 100 and 200 people well enough to have a conversation with them.

This part of your business is very nerve wracking: it can be quite scary because you are now having to put something out to market that could be rejected. I understand that, but it's more important to find out that no one is interested now, than further down the line. So to do that, we need to reach out to our network and ask them "do you know someone like this?" For example, we have our second time author who is releasing a course. If you reach out to your network and ask them "Do you know of any second time authors who are looking to build a course around their second book?" 95% of them are going to ignore you. The last 5% is going to be a mixture of people who will respond to you saying that they don't know anyone, or that they know someone or that they are that person. At this stage you don't need hundreds of leads; you need one sale to prove this works.

The thing most people get wrong about referrals is that a referral is something you can accelerate and control. Most people believe a referral is generated by the goodness of a customer's heart or our reputation in our network. When in fact it's something you should be asking your customers for and your network. Gyms that are successful do this well, incentivising and promoting referrals in order for a reward. If you get good at generating referrals now when you're first starting, you'll find it much easier to generate referrals and greenfield leads in the future.

So we're going to go out to our network and ask them if they know anyone that we can look to work with and start generating some leads for your business. There's a lot to be said for advertising and networking, as well as group promotion and creating content. However, most people treat those as sales procrastination or sales avoidance. There is nothing that will make a sale faster than making a sale. It's not even that uncomfortable; it's purely because you haven't done it before that it makes it seem scarier than it is.

"But Mike, don't I need a website, brochure, product, portfolio and experience before I go to market?" The short answer is no. First of all, you should already have your 10,000 word killer blog post. Having some kind of website with a contact form at least and that content on there is a hundred times more important than having a services page that lists out all the products and services you deliver. Thinking of clever copy and titles for products that don't exist is more wasted effort than going out and having conversations with prospects and leads. And the funny thing about your network is that they want to help you. This is why we are going out to our current network, rather than advertising to our new market.

You don't need a portfolio because you've written the blog content. And to build any kind of product or system before selling it, is a massive gamble and could result in huge losses. The reality is the business idea that you have now, as a product, will almost certainly shift and adapt as you begin to talk to customers and have more conversations with them. The danger in building a product before you sell it, is that you are making the assumption that customers want exactly what you are offering. I've made this mistake a couple of times, creating apps and software for a market, assuming they would love it. Only for it to fall on deaf ears. But when I've had conversations with prospects and potential customers, asking them what their problems are, I've been able to offer a solution which is suitable to them and didn't require any work from me upfront to develop it.

I'll give a template later in the book, but what we're doing is reaching out to our current network and asking them if they know anyone that we can work with. Most businesses when they ask for referrals will make one big mistake.

Telling people what you do is a mistake

As we've mentioned before, the second law of selling marketing funnels is that "who you work with, is more important than what you do". I see a lot of requests for referrals asking if I know anyone who needs a designer, or developer or copywriter. I applaud the initiative asking for a referral, but it's harder for me to recommend you to someone when I only know what you do. Telling me what you do doesn't give me enough to work with.

Frankly, I know loads of developers, designers, copywriters and other digital creatives. And chances are, they're probably as good as you if not better. Even if they're not, it doesn't matter because I'm not going to give you anyone in my network's contact information when all I know about you is that you *do* something. This is true of all lead generation from a cold/introduction standpoint by the way. When you introduce yourself to someone and tell them *what* you do, you're killing the flow of conversation. Start telling people <u>who</u> you work with. It's easier to remember and more likely to generate referrals.

Tell people who you work with

In Chapter 1: Audience, we talked about our niche statement builder. It tells people who you work with; the types of results you get them; the problems you solve and maybe a few characteristics about that person.

We work with physical product retailers who need a physical store, who want to double the number of locations they have in order to expand into new cities.

We work with email lists of over 10,000 people who want to launch new apps to the market and land a 7 figure launch week.

We work with authors who want to produce a course on their second book and sell it for 6 figures a year.

Every single one of these could be 'done' by a marketer, copywriter, business coach or...funnel builder. But, law 1 of selling marketing funnels is "If you want to sell marketing funnels, don't talk about marketing funnels".

It's a running joke in my circle of friends and my office that no-one really knows what I do. "Something to do with funnels and marketing and sales maybe? I know he's written a book.." Partly that's my fault, I haven't told people that I know, what I do (an important lesson - do your friends, or spouse or partner, know what you do?) And partly that's because what I do is not that important. I run a business. That's about it.

But if you ask them *who* I work with, I think the answer "marketing companies or agencies" is a lot easier. I work with marketing agencies to increase their prices and sell more of their services. *How* I do that is unimportant, *who* I work with is important. Overall, most people understand a lot about the world if you'll give them a chance. However, telling people what you do shuts their brain down. They want to refer you to their friends and colleagues; they just don't know how. If you give them a reason and a chance to refer you, they'll gladly tell people about you. And that reason is helping them understand WHO you work with. Most people don't know who would use a designer or developer or funnel builder or marketer or any other job title. What does a Financial Controller do? What kind of bullshit title is Chief Innovation Officer? What's a General Manager on a normal day? We're all caught up in our titles and jargon and industries so much that we assume others know what we do. The assumption is that we know how other people would benefit from someone like us in their lives.

This is where the disconnect is. When we ask for referrals, if we tell people what we do, we're making a huge leap that they'll know exactly what we do and most importantly *who* would benefit from the introduction. And that's the key - we need to make it clear *who* would benefit from knowing us. Instead, if I tell people the job title that I work with, instead of telling them my job title, it's easier to make a connection. Even if my network doesn't know any marketing agencies or funnel builders, it's easier for friends to recommend me when they know who I work with.

Your message and marketing and brand will spread much quicker when people know who you work with. So, our referral request will tell people who we work with and how it benefits them.

Ask to give, not get

The second part of the referral process is to ask to give something to referrals, rather than asking to get a call or appointment. This is one of the reasons the long form, killer blog post exists. Once you have a piece of content like that, you instantly position yourself as an expert with something to give rather than asking for something in return.

It doesn't have to be a blog post. You can have any piece of content like a video or worksheet. But it's important to know that people will be far more open to referral introductions if you aren't asking for a call. You're also more likely to book calls with prospects when you've given them something upfront first.

There's nothing wrong with asking to give a presentation or show people how you can help, but it's less of a stretch when you've already given them something upfront. Another idea is to invite them to a private social group on LinkedIn, Facebook etc. and offer that in the referral.

Referral plan

This is a high level overview of the referral plan we're going to use.

1. Make a list of as many people as possible that we could reach out to:
   a. Facebook
   b. LinkedIn
   c. Email
   d. WhatsApp
   e. Twitter

Write an email/message (using our template) that tells people who we work with and that we have a piece of content and ask them if they know anyone that we might/could work with.

2. Receive a 2% - 5% response rate and follow up with all referrals.

3. Talk to the referrals, offer them the content, book a call.
4. Qualify and sell (next chapter).

Make a list

You'll need a list of people that you know well enough to *ask* them if they know anyone you could work with. Remember, we're going to our network with a message of "I work with these kinds of people" not "I do this kind of work". So we need them to know who we are but don't limit it to just friends and family. Talk to ex-colleagues, customers, people you've met at networking events etc. You'll want a list of around 100 - 200 people. If you can do more, awesome, but don't stress yourself. This is as much about building up the habit as it is about starting to get momentum.

Don't feel you have to make a list of each person and their contact details. What we want is a rough outline of what platforms you have available and who you could contact on each platform. Have a look through your connections and write out the total number of people who you could send the below email/message to.

For example, you might have over 1000 connections on LinkedIn, but only 100 of them are worth reaching out to. Facebook might have fewer connections but closer friends so you're happy asking them if they know. If you have email addresses - great, but this *isn't* a cold sale or a lead generation call. It's asking if they *know* anyone who fits what you're looking for.

Write an email/message

Here's the message you need to send to your network to start building a list of potential customers and leads.

Partner outreach email 1

Hi [name]
I just wanted to reach out and ask if you know anyone in the [niche] space? We've been focusing our efforts in the [niche] market by helping [niche] with [characteristic] get [result]/solve [problem].
If you know anyone at all in that space, we'd love to get their contact information and just to talk to them. Thanks for reading.
Cheers
[your name]

Partner outreach email 2

Hey [name]!
Do you know anyone in the [niche] space? We've just published a crazy long, high quality blog post on how [niche] with [characteristics] can solve

[problem]/get [result].

If you know anyone that might be interested in reading this, I'd gladly pass it on. Or if you're happy to share it, that would mean a lot to me.

Thanks again, catch up soon.

[name]

You can download a copy of these at sellyourservice.co.uk/fivefigurefunnels. You need to start telling people *who* you work with and the more people that know, the faster you'll see leads come in.

Won't people be pissed off?

Your friends and network absolutely will not be pissed off. You're just asking if they know anyone who fits the criteria you're after. Frankly, this is not only how a large chunk of your sales in future will be made (because this IS the referral process), but it's also how people find partners, husbands, wives, girlfriends, boyfriends, gym buddies, running groups, accountants and every other type of relationship. Anyone who is pissed off at you asking for their help was never that close to you, or isn't worth hanging around. If anything, people will feel bad that they can't help you more.

Isn't this just cold calling?

Sure, I can understand why you'd think this looks like cold calling. However, it has a massive difference. It's not cold calling because the next email/message you send to the potential lead will mention your connection and referral. Cold calling (which by the way, there isn't anything wrong with), is when we scan through some data and just start dialling people who we think will be interested. Don't get me wrong, I loathe bad cold calling messages and emails; it drives me nuts. But, there is something to be said for a proper cold introduction and when it's done well, it can work. We however are using a referral to introduce us to their friend.

I don't think I'll be very good at this.

Honestly? At first, no, you probably won't be. But that's a good thing. It's better to be bad at it now before you start gaining some momentum. Think about it, let's say you send 10 emails and you realise there is a typo in the email and it doesn't really sound like it's coming from you. Isn't it better you learn that now, rather than going full-hog, sending it to hundreds of people and realising then?

You'll naturally get better at this over time. Your results will improve and the great thing about improvement is that you're making it better for the next people who you do reach out to. This is similar to product improvement. You want to get started now, and do a bad-ish job at it, because by definition

109

you'll get more people in the future so don't you want them to have the best experience possible? Besides, there is nothing so awful that it can't be fixed or changed. You're doing something new and it'll be uncomfortable, but that's where progress is made.

2% - 5% response rate

Roughly speaking, Peralto's Principle of 80/20 will be in play here, but twice. First, of all the people you send this message to, asking if they know someone, 80% won't ever get back to you. Of the 20% that are left, 80% of that will say they don't know anyone but they'll keep you in mind. 20% of the 20% will get back to you and say they might know someone, or they are that person. If we email 100 people, 80 of which will never get back to us (80%). Of the 20 people left, 80% of them (16) will say they don't know anyone. This leaves us with 20% of 20, or around 4 people who will respond with something positive. This is a good thing.

First, you probably don't have the resources or bandwidth to deal with too many leads and referrals right now. Let's keep the numbers low and automate and scale the sales and marketing stuff later. Secondly, even those who have never got back to you, everyone you sent that email to now knows who you work with. And as we've demonstrated before, this is 100x more powerful and important than telling people what you do.

Talk to the referrals

Anyone who gets back to you with some kind of lead or referral needs to be thanked and followed up with. You could receive responses ranging in detail. From "yeah I know someone", to "Hey Mike! Yeah I can help. I have Steve, Andy and Sarah who all fit your bill. I'll send them a note and CC you to the email! We should go for lunch soon!"

What *you* need is contact information and a name. Thank the people who get back to you and ask them for the contact information and name. If they've given you everything already, great. Thank them and work on following up with the lead. I can't stress this enough, *thank* people who have helped you. Now we need to get in touch with the lead. The #1 goal for reaching out with the lead is to get them on a call. When you reach out to your leads or referrals, use a template like the one below:

Referral lead email 1

Hi [name]
I got your details from [network name] and they mentioned that you're in the [niche] space.
I work with the [niche] market by helping [niche] with [characteristic] get [result]/solve [problem].

I'd love to show you how [niche] with [characteristics] can solve [problem]/get [result]. I've got a brilliant blog post/ebook/framework that I'd love to share with you.

Are you the best person to send that to?

Cheers

[your name]

No pressure, no hard sell. Also, notice that I'm not telling them what we do. Just what *they* would want as the niche. I'm also qualifying them by asking if they're the best person to send the resource to. I want them to get back to me with something like "yes, please send that over". I'll also CC the referrer to the email or include them in the message if I can.

When they get back to you, if they *aren't* the right person, get the right person's details and repeat. When you're speaking to the right person, you want to get them on a call.

Referral lead email 2

Hi [name]!

Thanks so much for getting back to me. I've attached the free report/ebook/blog post.

When I spoke to [network name], they told me that you might be interested in our process for helping [niche] with [characteristic] get [result]. I'd love to show you that process and how it would work for a business like yours. When can I get 12 minutes of your time to show you how we help [niche] with [characteristic] get [result]?

I'm free next Tuesday at 2pm, 3pm and 5pm. Just let me know.

Cheers

[your name]

I believe the #1 reason people fail to get on calls with leads is because they don't take enough control and initiate the meeting. You might think that gently offering a call if they want, with no pressure or set times, gives them freedom to choose and they appreciate that. Unfortunately, you're wrong. Choice takes energy and unless you give people exact boundaries to work with, they'd rather not get back to you at all. It's 100x easier to look at my calendar and see times that aren't there, rather than look for when is available. Besides, *you* want the call - they don't really. You need to be seen to do everything you can to get on that call.

What if they don't respond?

At any point, either after email 1 or 2, if they don't get back to you, keep following up. Ask your referral for their number and try calling them. Connect with them on LinkedIn, follow them on Twitter and subscribe to their channel. Stalk them. Be in front of them as much as you can. They won't get pissed off. You're in a hurry to help them; that's why you're pursuing them!

Qualify and sell

The entire next chapter is dedicated to qualifying customers and selling to them, so we're not going to cover too much here. Right, you've got on a call with the lead and now comes the sales process. Dread it, run from it, destiny arrives all the same. Sales cannot be avoided and no matter how great your marketing is or how incredible your product is, someone is going to have to sell it.

But remember, we've discovered benefits to your services and products that are good. Really good. And you deserve to get them out there. Customer's deserve to have them. All we can do now is accelerate the rate at which you attract leads and attention.

Regular content

Absolutely nothing will increase your authority and gain you more attention in the marketplace than posting regular content to a platform. Nothing can beat the perceived value and credibility of someone who repeatedly and consistently publishes ideas, gives away helpful information and provides content for free.

Above all else, content is a platform to test your ideas. The more I have blogged, videoed and podcasted my ideas, thoughts, processes and stories, the clearer I've become on my purpose, mission and values. The strength of my niche in sales training for funnel builders is deepened by content creation. I didn't magically stumble across combining sales training and funnel builders; it started as just helping all kinds of digital creative businesses, including WordPress agencies, graphic designers and copywriters.

However, over time as I focused on what I enjoyed, what I was good at and what people paid attention to (or paid me for), it became clear that sales training for funnel builders was my sweet spot. I wish I could tell you a faster route to generating massive levels of authority, attention and clarity within your own business, but I can't teach what I haven't done. And in my case, the way that I became so clear on my business was through creating a lot of content.

There is of course a fast track way - spending a lot of money, but past experiences have shown us that no amount of money can replace history. I was recently at the Mastermind where one of the big takeaways was "you can't fast track history". What this means is publishing a lot of content over a long period of time will always serve you and your business well. You can't pay to fast track it. And even if you do have the money to fast track authority and attention in the marketplace, you probably still won't be as clear on your niche for a variety of reasons. If I gave you a niche today, it wouldn't work. Partly because it might not be something that you resonate with, but also because creating a niche from nothing inspires fear. We've covered off the reasons why you shouldn't be afraid to have a niche, but the reality is part of you probably still will be afraid to commit to such a small segment of the market. However, writing and publishing and creating content gives you feedback and slowly helps you commit to a niche.

In my second book, Universe Fuel, I talk about how universe fuel is built with momentum and returns more than is put in. Eventually, the single blog post that you publish per week, or the single YouTube video you share, will attract more attention and grow your authority than your entire previous channel combined. I now attract more traffic to one blog post in a week than my entire blog attracted in its first years. I have essentially automated attention and authority in the marketplace.

Platforms

"But which platform should I focus on Mike?" This is a great example of how messy, convoluted and oversaturated the market is. Firstly, everyone will tell you that you should be doing videos. I seem to be telling you that blog posts might be the way to go. Then someone else will tell you that you absolutely must do a podcast. I'm going to let you in on a secret, it doesn't matter which platform you use.

I love Gary V and it's all well and good saying "be on all platforms all the time; you never know which one is going to take off" but while that might work to scale from 7 figures a year to 8 figures a year, it's not a sensible way to invest your already limited time and resources. A bit like how I say "there is no profit in a niche, just in your dedication to a niche"; it's the same with content platforms. There isn't one platform that will outperform another if you dedicate yourself to it.

Whatever platform you choose, like most pursuits, 90% of people will give up within the first 6 months. Of the 10% left, 90% will give up in the first year or two. This is why I take platform recommendations with a pinch of salt. I've seen time and time again people evangelise about the power of podcasting and YouTube and blogging, only to see they've been doing it for less than one year. It's like when your friend becomes a vegan or starts going to the gym, all of a sudden they talk about it non-stop but they've only been doing it 45 minutes. There is no fast track to success and anyone who has been on any platform for a long time will tell you how much hard work it is.

Google isn't dead; YouTube isn't dead; blogging isn't dead; podcasting isn't dead - we're *just* getting started with these platforms. It's just easier to say something is dead when you don't have the grit to stick with something for over 3 years to see it grow. When I interviewed Sarah Turner from The Unmumsy Mum, she told me that she gets loads of people (women mainly) asking her about becoming a blogger and an author. Sarah has over 300k Instagram subscribers, tens of thousands of readers of her blog, multiple best selling books and remains top of book charts for parenting and family. People want that lifestyle and that success, and Sarah tells them "it's easy'. You just don't make any money for 5 years and don't get paid for it. And write every day." When people hear the truth about the book, blog and social, and how much hard work it is, they say "it's easy for Sarah, she caught the Mummy Blog fad before it got too big." This is bullshit. Sarah posted and wrote and published for *years* before she achieved mainstream success. It's got absolutely zero to do with the platform or timing; it's all to do with grit and sticking it out.

All platforms have advantages and disadvantages. All platforms make life easier in one respect and harder in another. For example, YouTube is the second largest search engine on the internet, with roughly ⅓ of internet traffic going through it. Videos make for amazing content and can be much faster to create and start a following. However, it's not *your* audience and if YouTube decides to change their terms (like they have done again and again and again), you could be left up a creek without a paddle.

On the other hand, keeping your content on your site is a smart play. It's on your turf and if you need to change hosts or even platforms, no worries, just switch it over and no one knows any different. I think blogging is easier because you can do it anywhere. It's quiet and you can play around with your copy more easily. However, it's also a ball-ache to write all the time and can create massive publishing phobia. It's also harder to build a following because you have to drive traffic, promote and write a lot of content.

In terms of sticking to a platform and choosing one, you're going to fall in and out of love with whatever you choose. So don't think you've made the wrong choice just because it starts to feel like hard work or things don't seem easy or simple all the time. There is something to be said for video and using that video to turn into audio and then written content (through content repurposing). Nevertheless, in my experience I've found that you should choose a platform you want to stick to and work on every day (yes, every day).

Don't think of your content (when you start out) as a honeypot to attract traffic. Yes, your videos or blog or podcast will eventually attract traffic and new subscribers and audience. However, to start with we need to treat it like an archive for all your ideas and answers. Chances are you're asked the same 10 questions over and over, in person or via email. Or, you see the same questions in forums and groups online. Rather than typing out the same answer again and again, creating content is a great way to answer a question and appear like you know what you're talking about. People are seen as experts when they have content that answers common questions. Treat your content like an archive and the traffic and new subscribers will come in time.

Consistency

More important than the media is consistency. At a bare minimum you need to create one piece per week, and ideally, you'll be creating something every day. Lots of people get too focused on how many pieces they should create and in truth, you could do something once a month IF you put the work into promoting and sharing your content. I'm a firm believer that if something is worth doing, it's worth doing 1000 times. And the process of gaining attention in the market is absolutely reliant on the market seeing you do something 1000 times. That 1000 times however, must include the creation, publishing and *promotion* of the content piece. It's not enough to put something on a blog or YouTube channel and just wait. Yes, a big part of this journey is patience, but it's patience on results not on the effort required.

In my book Universe Fuel I talk about how you need to give 10 to get 1. You need to give 10 units of work, to get 1 result out. For example, if everyone in your industry puts out 1 piece of content, you need to do 10. If people in your industry give 1/10 for effort with their content, promotion and creation, you need to give 10. What does 10 look like? It's going deeper than most people are bothered with. Yes, good enough is good enough and publishing something at 60% done with typos, editing errors and bad sound is 100x more effective than never publishing it, but that's just the *start*. People mistake 'published beats perfect' for an excuse to just put something out and leave it, when most people don't even get started on the real hard work of promoting, sharing and creating their content.

There are 3 parts to any content creation process: Creating, publishing and promotion.

Creation is the act of bringing the content idea into the world and writing, filming or recording the piece. Then editing, cutting content and forming it into something that people will want to watch, read or listen to. Typically, writing a blog post or filming a YouTube video is the part that most people focus on. Our education system massively over-values perfection, creation and completing work. So much so that we carry that forward into adulthood and think of the market as something that 'marks' or examines our work and deems it worthy. This couldn't be further from the truth when there are two more stages that people neglect after creation. Publishing and promotion.

Publishing is the act of putting the media on a platform where it can be consumed. Creation is writing the blog post or book, publishing is putting it on a blog or platform. Publishing is it's own monster and in my opinion, harder and more work than creation. If you've written a blog post, a book, recorded a video or a podcast and you *haven't* pressed the publish button, you don't have any content. 1000 unpublished articles does not equal 1 published article. Publishing is setting up tags, categories, thumbnails, typography, descriptions and playlists. It's the process of taking what has been created and making it as attractive to consume as possible. It's also about making it easy to find and discover for other people. Publishing is where most big YouTubers spend their time. Have you noticed how the top YouTube channels don't *seem* to be doing anything particularly different or unique? Hell, some of their content is super boring. But it gets views and that's what matters. It's because they spend more time working on their publishing game than their creation game. There are tons of blogs out there with loads of traffic that I think give pretty weak advice. So, why do they get so many visitors? Because they focus on publishing and the next stage.

Promotion is taking what you've got, once it's published, and sharing it with as many people as possible. As a rule, for every hour creating a post, you want to spend 4x that on promotion. That's right. Each article that takes 1 hour to create, you need to spend 4 hours on promotion. A big chunk of that can be used in the publishing process, doing keyword research and setting up tags and descriptions. But you absolutely must share it with an audience. Putting a few tweets out there doesn't count. Like I mentioned, that's what everyone else does. That's 1/10. You need to go 10/10.

Ideally, you'll share it with your audience on Facebook and LinkedIn as well as your own email list. Even if you've only got 5 followers and 10 email addresses, share it. Then, going in social groups and becoming known and liked and trusted with that group. Do this *before* posting any content, even in the comments section of a post. As someone who runs a Facebook group, nothing winds me up more than someone joining and then posting a blog post in there 8 minutes after joining the group. However, if you get to know the people in the group and become a known face, they'll not only want to see content from you, they'll *ask* to see content from you. Spend time building trust and awareness inside other groups slowly and methodically and consistently. Do little and often for a long time, eventually, you'll have a group of people who want to hear from you. Of course, you should be building your own audience too.

Content ideas

I have a blog post[4] talking about how to come up with a ton of content ideas. I also talk a lot about content creation at scale in my book From Single To Scale. Content idea creation is a really fun exercise and good in groups too. And I've got a few more ways to think of content ideas below.

100 problems

Just list out 100 problems that your customers have. Simple as that. Write 100 problems that they face in their business and life that they're dealing with.

---

[4] https://sellyourservice.co.uk/killer-content/

Don't overthink it, just write and get it down on paper. Don't bullshit me and say you can think of 100 - write them down. Notepad, type, bullet list, it doesn't matter. Just think of 100 problems that your customers have and you can fix.

Ask your audience/customers

My favourite method of getting content ideas is to ask my audience: What stresses them out? What do they want to learn more about? What are their goals in the next 90 days? I ask my email list, my Facebook group and my coaching clients. I'll ask people in person and take photos of whiteboards or record questions during talks. There *are* patterns, and people ask the same questions which is why I phrase the question differently each time, talking about stress, thinking, learning, desires and goals.

Most common questions

What are the most common 10 - 20 questions you're asked? Record or write up the answer and refer people to them. Also, what questions *should* people be asking? What are they taking for granted or not asking at all?

Sales copy

If asking people is my favourite method, getting content ideas from sales copy is my second favourite. When you write sales copy, either as an email, landing page or product page, you are creating tons of great content ideas. From myths and misconceptions to the benefits, what you write up becomes 'how to' guides. Your sales copy is probably your best source of content that fits with your overall content funnel.

Script

I've already given you a script for a 10,000 word blog post in chapter 4, Authority, but I wanted to share my shorter script for getting content out there super quick. I use this as a script for blog posts, videos and podcasts. It's quick to fill out and means you can batch together lots of videos or posts at once. I particularly use this one for YouTube, but the process is interchangeable.

Content Script

This is the order that the script is presented and published in. I'll often record in this order too, but I will write and fill out the script starting with the Solution first, then the Problem, Myth, Hook and Question.

Hook

3 questions that draw the reader in. Focus on emotion and feelings, such as frustration and mixing it with curiosity.

E.g. Have you struggled to find a niche for your funnel business?

What does a niche look like in this hyper-competitive, over-saturated market?

Is your niche too broad or too narrow?

Bumper

5 second sting with logo. Use something like videobolt.net

Problem

What's the problem we're going to solve and that the viewer/reader is facing?

E.g. You just feel that the sale is slipping away.

Moved away from the process.

You don't know what to do next!

Myth

What is something that the reader/viewer believes which isn't true? What's standing in their way? And, what is the truth?

E.g. Proposals need to be long and complex, especially for marketing services and intangible services

Call to action

This is where you put a short CTA asking people to sign up, subscribe or download etc. Just before we get to the solution.

E.g. I've got some free training below on How to choose a niche for your funnel business: http://bit.ly/2KVn2VG

Solution

What are 3-7 learning points that teach people how to get the result, overcome the problem and fix it? For example:

- Spend time asking questions, not selling.
- Start with the solution that you would provide.
- Use a template.
- Write out the benefits of that solution.
- Tell them the problems they are facing.
- Include a timescale and investment page.

- Include a case study.

Question to audience

How do you want your audience to interact with your content? Do you want them to comment or share or tweet you? Ask a question and tell them how to get involved.

E.g. Which one of these mistakes do you see customers make? Let me know in the comments.

Product call to action

Another CTA or a repeat of the first one. Maybe a product or sale CTA. E.g. Coaching trial £1

20 second end screen

When publishing on YouTube you need a 20 second end screen to allow for further videos and to show an 'end screen'. This is a place to keep the viewer in your channel. With blog posts it's a good place to recommend another blog post.

Publishing Template

This publishing template gives a brief overview of how I publish YouTube content or podcasts. It's still important for blog posts but will probably be included in any blog content automatically.

Title

Catching, interesting title with a benefit and curiosity.

E.g.. Only amateurs worry about traffic (do this instead).

You must see there 5 ways to easily grow your email list.

WARNING: Stop writing blog content! It's killing your business.

Description

The description, particularly for YouTube videos, is extremely important. YouTube isn't a video platform or a social media platform, it's a search engine. So we need to give as many indicators as possible keywords that we want to appear for. And the description is one of the best places to do it. It's also a good place to put links to blog posts, squeeze pages, products and further content. Don't ever stuff your description with keywords because YouTube penalises against that. I'll usually repeat the title with the keywords as the first line in the description, followed by the call to action link and then a short description repeating some of the keywords I want to rank for.

E.g. How to write a marketing funnel proposal *** Marketing funnel proposal template: *https://betterproposals.io/proposal-templates/marketing-funnel-proposal-template*

I'm going to share with you the marketing funnel proposal template that is responsible for over $94 million worth of sales in 2018 alone. My friends at Better Proposals use my marketing funnel proposal template and I will show you how I write marketing funnel proposals for my customers. I love writing proposals because they're quick, easy and it means that someone is probably going to buy from me. I'm going to show you the marketing funnel proposal template I use, how I write proposals for my marketing funnels, and the marketing funnel proposal conversion hack that works with almost every customer.

Tags

Tags: the final part of any publishing process. The trick with tags is to narrow down and be specific about what you want to rank for. Don't try and spread your bets with lots of different tag words. Instead, try to focus on variations along a theme.

E.g. Marketing funnel proposal, How to write a marketing funnel proposal, How to write a funnel proposal, funnel proposal, how to write a proposal, better proposals, better proposals marketing funnel template, better proposals marketing funnel proposal template, marketing funnel proposal template

Summary

- Focus on who you work with not what you do when generating referrals
- The amount of sales and leads you generate will be DIRECTLY proportionate to the amount of effort you give to your attention
- Flip the sentiment and think about it as giving attention to a cause/audience as much as generating attention for yourself
- No other period in history has allowed anyone and everyone to generate attention as easily and cheaply as today

ACTION

Of all the chapters in this book, this was my favourite. I believe people don't like sales for the same reason they fear intimacy. We're taught to take care of our own tasks and we're taught to work in groups and communities. But we're seldom taught the dynamics of trust, confidence and communication between just two people. When you see how sales can benefit the person buying, you'll never fear your sales calls ever again.

Book calls

The goal now is to start booking calls. This is where you're going to start making traction and also where most people start to find excuses not to have conversations. Again, ABS - anything but sales.

But you are ready and you're in the best possible position. You've got a niche that you care about and want to work with. You've got a price point that is profitable and is justifiable. You've got a great product that is scalable and sellable. You've built a little authority around a subject with a great piece of content. And you know how to attract attention in the marketplace. You might have already generated a few referrals; you've got everything you need. Now we need to book some calls.

Around this point it can get a little murky and unclear what we're looking for. So I want to break down the steps that we're going to take, ending in a sale.

1. Initial lead enquiry
2. Qualify
3. Growth session
4. Proposal
5. Presenting
6. Closing
7. Turning objections

8. Leading up

Initial lead enquiry is where a prospect expresses interest in working with you. This could be asking to get on a call with you, emailing you, asking for prices or some kind of communication. If they've downloaded a lead magnet or free report and joined your email list, that isn't really a lead enquiry, but that's why you want to get people on a call and talk to them.

Qualify means to see if they have the means and will pay, and what their goals are. Essentially, you're looking to see if you're a good fit, if they can afford you and what they want. A deep dive or audit is how you learn more about the business and the situation they're in. It gives you the best indication as to what you need to fix in order to help them.

Proposal is the offer you make to the lead, usually as a written document that outlines what their future is going to look like and how much it'll cost. Presenting is the process of taking the customer through the proposal and getting them to sign up. Closing is how you get them to exchange their resources for your resources, usually getting them to sign a contract and pay a deposit. You also need to turn objections, which is an excuse the lead gives before they buy. And finally, you follow up with those people that you couldn't close on the day, which is to say you send reminders, emails and make phone calls to make the offer a few times until they say yes.

A few notes before you start is always a good idea: It's important to know that the 'sales' process E.g. the bit where you're showing how great you are and how much you can help, happens *before* the proposal. The proposal doesn't sell anything. The proposal is a closing tool. It's like a receipt or a programme for a play. It outlines what's going to happen, but you've already bought the product or ticket.

The sales process is two things:

1. Sales is a transference of enthusiasm.
2. Sales is working out if it makes sense for two parties to work together.

You must be enthusiastic about what you're selling and what you're delivering. You must also be enthusiastic about the customer, their situation (or at least enthusiastic about helping) and about the future they could have. You are also working out along the way if it makes sense for both the lead and yourselves to work together.

And right now, you need to book calls. You need to get people on the phone, Skype, Zoom, Whereby or whatever you use and start qualifying them. Essentially, you need to have conversations with people and ask them as many questions as you can. It's *easy* when someone emails you and wants to get on a call. That's super easy because they're coming to you. The power is still in your hand. And most funnel builders (in fact, most businesses in general), believe that the key to increasing sales and improving lead generation, is to get more people to call you. While that might be the goal, it's also never really going to happen like that - at least not for the reasons you think.

I don't know what the explanation is or what to call the phenomenon, but I have seen time and time again, that the business who is willing to contact leads and prospects first, and be willing to get on a call, eventually become overwhelmed (in a good way) with leads coming to them first. It's like the act of going out and finding leads yourself proves that you can handle it and then you'll have more leads come to you.

Those businesses that refuse to meet the universe halfway and reach out to leads first, are never rewarded with more people interested in contacting them because they haven't demonstrated that they want it enough. And of course it's easy to complain that lead generation both inbound and outbound doesn't work. It's a perverted methodology but it's also been shown to exist time and time again.

How I book calls

I believe the reason people don't want to get on a call is because they don't know what they'd say - either to get people to book a call or even on the call. The rest of this chapter will tell you exactly what you need to say. You probably need a call booking system first. I found it 100x easier to ask people to get on a call with me if the process was automated.

I use Calendly.com to send people a link such as *calendly.com/mikekillen/book* to book a call with me. Calendly connects with my Google Calendar which runs my schedule, and I tell Calendly only to allow calls on Tuesdays, Wednesdays and Thursdays between 2pm and 5pm. You can of course, set any times and dates that you want.

When I'm emailing a prospect or lead, I'll offer to get them on a call and I'll send them that link so they can book a time that suits them. Leads who ask to get on a call with me will be sent that link and if I'm talking with someone, and I think we should get on a call, I'll send them that link too.

It's not critical to have Calendly. Of course there are loads of different apps which do essentially the same thing. And it's not even critical to have a booking app. Simply asking people to get on a call and having a conversation with them can usually be enough. It's just a matter of managing your own time so that other people don't take up all of your time. I recommend setting aside half a day a week and seeing if you can just fill that time up with conversations and leads. In my experience, I've found that asking to get on a call with someone to ask more about their business and they ask you questions yields pretty good results, compared to asking to get on a call, so you can show them something.

"Hey Mark, I'd love to get on a call and ask a little bit more about your business. And if you've got any questions, it'll be a good chance for you to ask them. Are you free next week for a call? It will only take 25 minutes. How about next Tuesday at 3pm?" I have always found that offering someone a time and a date is the best way to get a call. It's much easier for someone to say yes or no to a time and date, compared to having to think of a time themselves. I've always found people more receptive to getting on a call when I tell them when the call is. If they are open to a call but can't do any of the times or dates you have suggested, then send them a Calendly link.

As a rule Calendly booking links are fantastic for when the lead reaches out to you.

Lead enquiry

Let's say you have someone who has demonstrated some kind of interest. Maybe they've emailed you asking if you can help. Or they've signed up to your newsletter and you think it would be worth reaching out to them. Either way, someone has expressed some kind of interest in working with you. Now what?

Now, you need to get them on a call. If you've got a Calendly link set up like the example above, or some kind of calendar booking system, your job is to get as many people booked onto calls as possible. Typically, most leads will demonstrate interest by emailing you something like the below.

"Hey Mike, Mark sent me your details. He says that you might be able to help with our marketing. Are you able to give me a suggestion of your prices, or maybe we could meet for coffee?"

Your job is to get them on a call so you can have a conversation with them. However, you are not going to give away free consultation or give them a price upfront. You are also definitely not going for coffee! As I mentioned above another potential lead enquiry could be someone you want to reach out to. The process is actually the same regardless of how you get to this point. Let's say you've done some research on a prospect or potential customer and you think you could work with them. Your job is to still get them on a call. You want to try and get prospects on the phone whether they've reached out to you or you've reached out to them, so you can take them through the next stage, which is qualification.

Lead qualification

The number one mistake I believe funnel builders make when they have a new potential lead is to go straight into sales mode. It's funny really because I've met so many marketing agencies who don't like selling and think themselves above selling, but when they encounter a new lead or prospect, they go immediately into 'sales mode'.

This entire book is designed to help you sell more marketing funnels to your customers. I would be the last person to tell you that you shouldn't be trying to sell or doing everything you can to sell to customers. However, I also think that how you drive on a professional racetrack is going to be very different to how you drive your car to arrive at the racetrack.

You can't go straight into sales mode because frankly, you don't know enough about the customer. All too often, I see marketing agencies and funnel builders do everything they can to explain the features and benefits of their products to the customer, in order for the customer to make a decision whether they want to buy.

This is a real shame because that's not what you need to do at this point of the customer journey. What you need to do is qualify the lead. Whenever there is a new potential prospect or customer, try to refrain from immediately selling to them. Instead, you are going to work out if they have the means and ability to pay for you, and if you want to work with them.

When I first started my marketing funnel business, I was very hesitant to qualify customers in the way that I had been taught in my previous corporate marketing job. Even though I knew the value of lead qualification, my attitude was "beggars can't be choosers". That was until I was challenged by one of my mentors "Mike, do you still consider yourself a beggar?"

Instead of thinking about how your product is either exclusive or you can't work with people even though they might really need your help, I want you to think about resource allocation. This is not a case of excluding customers because you think you are above them. It's a case of understanding that you can only help so many people, and that it would be a waste of resources to help people that don't benefit from your expertise.

The five basic questions for qualifying a customer are as follows.

1. Can the customer afford me?
2. Can they afford to implement my advice?
3. Do I like them?
4. Can I get them extraordinary results?
5. Do they refer?

They need to build answers positively to all five of these questions. Arguably, question number three and four are perhaps more important. Unless you like working with them, no amount of money is going to make the project worthwhile. And if you can't get them extraordinary results no amount of money they spend will make them happy with working with you.

So through the process of initial lead enquiry and qualification, we need to be able to answer these five questions. You could just ask these questions, but customers have a way of telling you what you want to hear which is why you're going to ask five different questions. You're going to be asking them about their budget, who are the decision-makers, one of their goals, when do they want to start and who are they working with. Also known as BANTS.

Budget, Authority, Needs, Timescales and Suppliers. What's the budget? Who is the authority, also known as the decision-maker? What are their business needs, goals, problems etc? Whatever timescales for starting and achieving results? Who else are their suppliers and who are they working with? BANTS.

I've included a worksheet at sellyourservice.co.uk/fivefigurefunnels with all the questions you need to ask during the qualification call. This can be a 25-minute call via zoom or Skype but it doesn't need to be in person. All you're doing is running through this list of questions which I also give you below to understand if they are the right type of customer to work with.

Qualification Script

- What's the name of your business?
- What's your name?
- What's your email address?
- What's your role in the business?
- What's your phone number?
- What does your business do?
- What's your website?
- What are your top 3 goals for the business?
- What are you willing to spend to reach those goals?
- What are your top 3 problems or struggles?
- What are you willing to spend to solve those problems?
- How often do you create and publish content?
    - >How often?
    - >How much content do you have?
- Do you spend money on adverts or traffic?
    - >How much?
- Are you willing to spend money on advertising to drive new sales?
- How big is your audience online with Facebook, Twitter, YouTube etc?
- What kind of budget do you have for a project like this?
- What kinds of tools do you use at the moment?
- Are you the key decision maker?
    - N>Who else needs to know about the project?
- When are you looking to start the project?
- Have you worked with a scale agency before?
    - Y>Who are you working with/have you worked with?

- Why are you looking to talk to me and my team?
- When are you looking to start working?

These questions will help you get a better understanding about the customer's business. And make no mistake, qualifying the customer is absolutely vital to the rest of the sales process.

Higher conversions, short sale time

When you qualify customers, you will find that the conversion rate of your proposals and offers will be higher the more time you spend qualifying the customer. The more certain you are about the types of customers you can and can't work with, the more likely you are to find customers you want to work with.

If for no other reason, you should be qualifying your customers so that your proposals and offer rate is more likely to be accepted when you make them. This is for two reasons: First of all, it's because you have made the customer work for it. The second reason is that the more time you spend qualifying a customer, the better you will understand them. Customers do not buy marketing funnels because you have talked about marketing funnels. Customers buy marketing funnels because they have talked about their business.

The more questions you have asked your customers and the more they get to talk about their business the more likely they are to buy. This is because first of all you have learnt more about their business and will be able to sell to their real desires. But also, people trust people more when they are allowed to talk. Someone doesn't perceive you as an expert because you've talked about your business. People perceive you as an expert because you've asked questions about their business.

You don't have infinite resources

The second reason to qualify is that you can't afford not to. I don't doubt that every business in the world would benefit from spending time with you. I'm sure that every business would see some improvement after working with you. The truth however, is that you are not Google and you are not Coca-Cola. You don't have the resources to reach, sell, serve and respond to every business out there. You don't even have the resources to serve every business that gets in contact with you.

One of the reasons that funnel businesses fail where they needn't, is because they try to serve too many low value customers. A lot of the time customers simply aren't worth the hassle. As awful as this sounds, many of them simply won't get the results that they need and that you can provide.

In the first chapter we looked at our audience or niche essentially asking the question; Who benefits the most from working with us? You must stick to this answer if you want to find customers that benefit from working with you. For example, if you have two businesses approach you both with the same budget, but with different business models, who would you prefer to work with?

Business A

- Currently at 1000 sales a year, with each sale roughly £1000
- Approximately 2000 customers on their database
- Currently spending money on advertising
- Range of products from £10-£10,000

Business B

- Zero sales with a product worth £100
- Few hundred leads in their database
- Zero spend on advertising
- One product

Business A is doing roughly £1 million a year turnover and has lots of potential customers. They also have a range of products and are currently spending money on advertising. What this tells you is that they are selling already. If you were to increase sales by just 10%, that would be an extra £100,000 in revenue probably with a higher profit margin also.

Business B is doing zero in revenue. They don't have a range of products and they would have to sell 10 times the number of products Business A cells, in order to match revenues. If you generated £50,000 in sales for Business B, that would be a 100% increase in revenue. You would be essentially taking their business from 0 to 50,000 and you still wouldn't make as much money as you would in Business A.

This might look like a trick question but Business A is in fact the best business to work with. You would want to work with Business A more because it's easier to generate a higher level of return. As I mentioned above, customers are only happy with you when you are visibly getting them results. The problem is that even businesses who you help take from 0 to 50,000, will not see that as a massive improvement. I would also bet that I could get Business A a hundred thousand pounds in revenue faster than I could get Business B £50,000 in revenue. Everything about Business B might suggest it would benefit more but the numbers suggest Business A would benefit more.

Are they the right customer?

I can't answer this for you, but you'll have to make the decision based on the answers you get during the qualification calls. It's important to note that qualifying a customer is NOT selling to the customer. Your job is simply to find out "Can I help this customer and can they afford me?" Remember those 5 questions above?

1. Can the customer afford me?
2. Can they afford to implement my advice?
3. Do I like them?
4. Can I get them extraordinary results?
5. Do they refer?

You need the answers to these questions to be a "yes". You need to know that you're placing your time and resources in the best possible place and that you can get the customer great results. Qualification is where most businesses, especially funnel and marketing business, fall down because they believe they can help everyone. They can't. As I've outlined above, not all customers are created equal. There's nothing more disheartening than working with a customer and them blaming you for poor results when really they were setting you up for failure.

If they fit your criteria and if you believe they'd be a good fit, we need to move onto the next stage of the process. You don't even have to tell them this on the call. You could just wrap up the call and let them know that you'll be in touch. If you're absolutely 100% sure that you want to work with them, by all means end the call with further details or booking another call; don't feel that you have to give them an answer right away. I like to finish my calls with something like the below:

> *Mrs. Customer, thanks so much for answering all my questions. Your project certainly sounds very interesting. I want to make sure I've understood and digested all that you've given me, so if it's OK with you I'd like to review my notes and come back to you with what I think the best plan would be.*

Remember, you don't have to give them an answer straight away. They'll probably be very happy that you've suggested that because it shows you're clearly taking this seriously. If they have questions, feel free to answer them, but I hate giving out free consultation and some customers are just trying to get free information out of you. So, I have a pretty standard response for any questions that I don't want to answer.

Some pretty typical questions are:
- How much do you think this will cost?
- Have you got a portfolio?
- What kind of traffic tactics do you think you'll use?
- Should I be advertising on Facebook?

Firstly, at the top of the call, I'll tell them when this call is *ending*. "Just to let you know, I've got a call straight after this so I'll have to jump off at 11:25, is that ok?" Of course they always say that's ok; this gives you an easy option to end the call.

Secondly, if they do have questions and you want to either leave the call or not answer them, just say something like the following "Good question. I want to make sure that I fully understand your business and the project before I make any recommendations or send over appropriate case studies. What I'm going to suggest is that we might need to book another call to further go over your questions and ideas, how does that sound?"

Even if you already know that you don't want to work with them, the goal of this call is NOT to give away free information or consult them for free. If they've got questions, great, they'll still have them on the next call. When you've decided whether or not you want to work with them, use an email like the below:

Hey Miss. Customer
Hope you're well, thanks for your time earlier in the week.
What I think we need to do next is a deep dive into your processes where you are now and build out a strategy of what you want to do. I recommend one of our Growth Strategy Sessions to start with.
It's about a 2 hour process which we can easily do over a call. However, I'd probably get one of my team to lead you through the process. I want to make sure we offer the most useful solution and identify the order of priorities for you.
It's a £497 one off cost, which at the end will give a better insight to yourself and us on what to focus on next. After that, we'll build a strategy and 'Gameplan' for your automation that you can use, whether you continue to work with us or not.
Can I book in a Growth Strategy Session for you?
Speak soon!
[sign off]

What we're doing is positioning a second call (which is paid) to better understand the client's needs and their business. One of the biggest mistakes that funnel agencies make is giving away free consultation, even though giving away information for free is likely to *lower* your conversion rates. Instead, you should be paid for your insight and to understand as much as you can about the customer. The more you know about them and their business, the better the position you're in. Yes, some of your old customers might baulk at the idea of paying to talk to you, but your new, qualified customers will be fine with it.

The massive misconception that people have about a five figure funnel price tag, is that the £25,000 price is justified in the delivery of the funnel. It's not. The £25,00 or £100,000 or £1m price tag is justified and sold way before the project is even delivered. The more time you invest into the customer, understanding them and their business, the bigger the price tag on the back end. If a customer can't afford £497 for a strategy call, how in the hell are they going to pay the big bucks? You're an expert and you deserve to be treated as such, which is why we sell a growth session.

Growth session

A Growth Session is sometimes called a discovery call, strategy call or an exploratory call. This stage is where you dig into the customer in depth and identify what you're going to work on. You're also going to finally answer some of their questions and tell them what they need to work on and fix. This goes against most common reasoning and accepted wisdom for running an agency or business, but it works.

I often talk about "value based selling" and how we must move into a position of selling intrinsic value over features. Sell Futures, Not Features right? Those futures that we sell to customers are uncovered during growth calls like this. The value that you build up in the customer's mind is built during smaller interactions like this. You're also going to answer all their questions (or at least the most important ones) and you're going to be paid for it.

The growth session is a specialist consultant in a hospital, compared to a GP. The qualification is like a GP at a surgery who understands what you need help with. The specialist consultant is the person who will probably treat you but they also need to run further tests. You're going to dive deep into their business and pinpoint what needs to be addressed first.

Can I pay you after the call?

I used to get asked this a lot and frankly - no. Of course you can't pay me after the call. However, customers are a sensitive sort so we need to position paying upfront as the best option. I like to use something like this "Mr. Customer can I ask why you don't want to pay upfront?" Their response is usually something like "I've been burnt before or what if the call isn't good?" It's basically a trust thing. You just need to turn the objection like so "I totally understand your hesitation, I've also been burnt before.

And because of that I've got a 100% refund guarantee where if you think the call didn't help at all, I'll refund every penny of your investment." Most of the time they're happy with that, but occasionally some smart-ass likes to say "well if you're so sure, why don't we do the call and then if it's good I'll pay you?" It sounds like a trick question, something you can't answer. By this point, I'm already sure that I don't want to work with them, but for the benefit of the doubt, I'll respond with "Mr. Customer that's a fair point and in my experience, all the customers that we've worked with want to put skin in the game and show us how serious they are by putting up a tiny amount up front. It shows that they're serious about their business and that I should be too. Are you serious about your business?" Play the ego card and get them to pay. But frankly, anyone who quibbles over £500 isn't my type of customer.

The growth session is split into two halves. The first half is deeper questions and exploration of their business. The second half is offering advice on what they need to focus on and how to fix it. Interestingly, customers *don't* just want you to tell them the answer. They think they want that, and so do we, but they don't. It's like giving advice to a teenager, they probably don't even know what to do with it. Instead, what customers *really* want to hear is their own ideas.

Have you ever heard the saying "Do you want my advice or do you just want me to agree with you?" It's a common communication problem that many people fall into. Most of the time, what they really want to hear is "It's not your fault. You're doing everything right. You don't need to change. It's the world that's wrong."

In Gordon Ramsay's Kitchen Nightmares, 3 Michelin Star Chef Gordon Ramsay goes into restaurants and identifies what they need to change in order to get out of debt and run a successful business. Time and time again, you'll see the chefs and owners say "I think our food is pretty good" but when Gordon tastes the food, it's a miracle if he likes it. Even when Gordon clearly lays out what needs to change and that the food sucks, the chef or owner will adamantly refuse to believe that they need to change. Why? Because people don't want to be told what to do, they want to be told what they already believe. Of course ,this wouldn't work especially in the TV show Kitchen Nightmares because if Gordon just said "Yeah the food's great. I can't understand why you're so unpopular." While that might make the owner feel good, it won't solve any problems.

Even more typically, many business owners and entrepreneurs do want to hear your ideas and will even be appreciative of you telling them, but they won't implement them. Why? Because usually the advice giver suffers from 'over sharing' and gives way too many ideas and the listener doesn't do any of them. So, how do you tell someone what they need to do to solve the problems in their business, without them rejecting your ideas? It's simple, but quite dull. You make them think it's *their* idea.

When someone arrives at a conclusion themselves, they're far more likely to follow it through. They're also more likely to do it because it'll be one objective rather than dozens of ideas. Getting someone to arrive at their own conclusion is a delicate balance because it means you have to steer them in the right direction, but give them the freedom to get there. Let's look at an example:

A customer of mine, Jen, ran a successful interior design company. She sold her consulting and design skills and also had suppliers who could install furnishings and remodelling work if needed. She wanted to expand her business and take on more staff. Jen wanted to do less of the design work herself and feel like she was running a business, not just working in one. Jen was convinced that her website needed more traffic and she needed to advertise more. If she got more clients through the door, she'd be able to hire someone and move out of the business.

However, after a little exploration, I discovered that what she really needed, was a process. She needed a design process or system for her interior design that someone could follow if she did hire someone. The problem wasn't cashflow or money, it was efficiency. Any time Jen tried to hire someone she'd end up doing the work anyway because "the other person wouldn't do it as well as me." Hires would either be fired or leave because they weren't doing enough design work and they had become admin assistants.

If I straight up told Jen that she needed to create processes and documentation (which, as a funnel business is a frequent need for customers) she'd have rejected it. Even if she agreed with me, the motivation to do what someone else tells you is far lower than doing something that you believe will work. After running through a growth session with Jen and asking the right questions, eventually she realised that she needed documentation. When *she* had arrived at that conclusion, I was able to offer ideas and help her. If I'd have offered all my insight upfront and earlier, it would have fallen on deaf ears.

I want to share my growth session script or process with you, in order to better help you run a paid growth or strategy session with customers, so you can help them and position yourself as an expert. At the end of the first half of the call, these 4 questions need to be answered:

- What is their priority goal?
- Why do they want to make things better?
- What is their biggest problem?
- Where are they now?
- We might end up with a statement like the below.

So you want to increase revenue to £1m per year-
because you want to sell the business.
You currently have £650 000 in revenue.
And you're struggling with attracting new clients.

Growth session script
What's future do they want?
- What are their goals?
- 30 days, 90 days, 1 year, 5 years?
- Where do they want to be?
- What does a good day look like?
- Get them to describe a great day.
- How much wealth?
- How often do they work?
- What are they working on?
- Get as many goals as possible.
- What is their top #1 priority?

You must get a #1 goal from them, something they want to focus on. And now this is the critical part - why? Why is this goal important? Why is it number 1? Even if it sounds obvious like "increase revenue" or "get more clients", ask them why. Why do they want more clients? Why do they want more revenue or sales or exposure or traffic? Asking *why* cuts past what they think the solution is and digs into the driving motivation behind their business. When you ask people what their goals are, they'll usually tell you what they believe the solution is. The *goal* isn't to get more clients, it's to spend less time at the office. The goal isn't to increase revenue or traffic, it's to sell the business and retire. Only asking *why* will get us past what their ideas are and into something that we can work with.

Remember, deep down people want permission or confirmation that their idea is the right idea. They want someone else to validate what their goal is and to hear that their idea is a good idea. The problem of course is that many times, it's not a good idea. If the goal was to make £X so they can travel more or hire someone, and they categorically knew that they need more traffic, why not just buy more traffic? Saying they don't know how isn't a good enough answer because if they were 100% sure it was the right idea, they'd just hire a traffic person. Instead, they're talking to you because, even though they wouldn't admit it, they don't know what to do.

Get a list of reasons *why* their goals are important and get as many as you can. Then, after they've given you all their reasons, ask them what the #1 priority reason WHY is. Which 'why' is the most important why? And then repeat the process. Why is that why, the most important why?

The further down the 'why' path you go, the clearer the real goals become. People's true motivating goals aren't to get fit or make money, they're to feel accepted and valued or respected. When we get into those deeper motivations, we're getting closer to the reason they'll buy *anything*. We're getting clearer on the future they'll buy, not the features you have.

Once you've gone at least 2 levels deep with the why, list that main deep driving motivation down as the 'goal' and move on:

- More traffic
- More revenue
- More customers
- More products
- More sales
- What's the priority?
  - More revenue
  - Why is that the priority?
    - More cash flow
    - More freedom
    - Easier to hire and expand
    - What is the priority?
      - Easier to hire and expand
      - Why is that the priority?
        - Need to spend less time working with customers
        - Want to work fewer hours
        - Want to spend more time with the family
        - Looking to start a new business
        - What's the priority?
          - Work fewer hours

135

In this example above, the *actual* goal is to work fewer hours.

What's the condition they are in now?

Repeat back their goals and ask where they are in comparison. Repeat back the priority goals E.g. we need to increase revenue so we can hire people, because you want to work fewer hours.

- Ask them to describe a typical day.
- Ask them to describe how that typical day makes them feel.
- What aren't they happy with?
- What are they happy with?
- What do they want to change?
- What do they want to keep?
- What could be better?
- What could be faster or easier?
- What do they wish they had to do less of?
- What's not working?

Get as much depth and emotional words from the customer as possible. Record as many emotional words as you can. This is their life and they're telling you what they want to change. This is what I mean when I say customers will tell you what they want to buy.

It doesn't have to be as deep as the goals section. No need to go deep and into the why's and motivations. You just want to get a picture of where they are. What you repeat back will be a summary of their day and it'll help them feel like you care about them and their situation.

What's stopping them?

Repeat back their current condition. Highlight a few key areas that they're either not happy with or that they want to change. Summarise it and use emotional language. This shows you're listening.

- Why haven't they changed their day and gone after their goals?
- What's preventing them from having what they want? You might want to list out each goal and ask what's preventing them from having it.
- What problems can they see going after those goals?
- What are their fears?
- What have they tried before?

You're going to repeat the what/why loop as before, asking the customer what is their #1 priority problem and *why* is that their problem? What's the biggest problem/priority problem? Why is that the biggest killer? You'll go a few levels deep and eventually by this stage it'll become clear on what you need to work on. When you ask *why* haven't you fixed this, rather than just "what is the problem" you help the customer reframe the roadblock.

If you want more traffic, and that is the goal, when you ask "what's the problem?" they'll just say "we don't have enough traffic." It's like Gordon Ramsay in Kitchen Nightmare's again asking what the problem with the restaurant is and the owner or manager saying "we don't have enough customers." Yeah, no shit.

Repeat and prescribe

Here's the killer part. The prescription. You just repeat back their goals, problems and status quo. Ideally, you've offered almost NO information yourself. You've just asked questions, prompted them and recorded their answers.

If you repeat back their story, you'll do two things. Firstly, you'll show that you actually listen. Deep down, this is really what people want. People want someone to listen to them. Secondly, you'll give THEM clarity on their next move. Incredibly, helping people realise their own problems and goals lets them see with clarity, what they need to do. They'll think you're a genius if you do this. The sentence works like this:

Ok, it sounds to me like you want to [key goal], and at the moment you [current status]. But in order to get there you need to [first roadblock]. Does that sound right?

Customer: Yes! That's exactly it!

OK, so it sounds to me like you want to work fewer hours, and at the moment, you're working on all customer projects with no time to work on the business. In order to change this, we need to sort out your hiring process. Does that sound right?

If they say "No", it just means that you've got the wrong goal or roadblock. It's no big deal. Just ask them "what's the bigger goal or roadblock?" They'll complete the puzzle for you. They'll fill in the blanks and you just repeat back their words.

"Ok, so you want [goal 2] and at the moment you're [status quo]. But in order to get there, you need to address [roadblock 2]. Does that sound right?

Would you like some help with that?

That's all you need to ask. By asking "would you like some help with that" you're getting them to sell their own ideas, to themselves. Simple as that. They'll say yes. After they've agreed with your summary and assessment, asking them if they want help with what they've told you, they'll arrive at a conclusion themselves. This is how you get someone to sell their own ideas and then you can start offering advice they'll listen to. This is now where you enter the second part of the growth session.

After uncovering their main goals and problems, you will need to explain to them what they should be doing next. It's tempting to give all of your best advice and ideas on how to solve this problem. The tricky thing is balancing giving enough ideas to work with, but not so many that it's overwhelming. Again, customers might think that they want all of your best ideas, but in my experience I found focusing on one core idea to be far more effective. People are able to execute and plan on one idea, rather than being given too many.

How I like to start the next stage is to ask customer for their ideas on what they should do. Some will already have a clear idea on what they believe the solution is. Others might be completely blank and ask something like "isn't that your job?" Don't take any initial answers at face value. Most customers, as we talked about before, are really just looking for reassurance and that they're making the right decisions. So I like to ask if they have any ideas on how to fix this. I start making a list. It's worth noting one of the most powerful consultation and questioning techniques I know: The power of staying silent.

Let's say that you've identified the customer's top goal is to sell the business in five years. Their biggest problem at the moment is they have unpredictable and unsteady cash flow. If you now ask them "so what do you think you could do about that?" You need to stay silent after whatever initial answers they give. Whether they say "isn't that your job" or "I have absolutely no idea" or "we could just do more advertising", I want you to practice staying quiet after their initial answer. The power of silence after someone has given you an answer will often force them to think deeper and longer about their response.

This is not the time to justify why you're asking the question; it's not the time to reassure them that you will give them an answer as well; we need to let them arrive at the best decision for their business. The funny thing about asking for advice is that most people know, most of the time, what the right choices are. What they want is someone to agree with them. In our example above, the 'correct' solution would be to find a recurring revenue stream and increase sales and marketing. They may know that deep down, but might take a while to get there. Your job is not to necessarily give them answers, but to help them arrive at those answers. You'll then help them execute their final decision. Of course, with your professional expertise and your process which we've outlined above, you'll also have a clear idea on how to help the customer.

Let them get their initial answer out the way, then stay <u>totally silent</u>. They will search their brains for another answer that will get you to respond to them. No matter how awkward it feels, or how long you stay quiet, keep your mouth shut. Give them the space and time to think of another answer which satisfies you until they have given you a couple of really good suggestions. Just write down their answers and give them space. I'll sometimes leave them for five minutes just to think of ideas and then brainstorm them for the solution.

One of two things will happen: Either, they will make a suggestion that you agree with. For example, they might say something simple such as "We need to fix our recurring revenue." or "We need to increase sales and marketing." They might not have the exact process to do that, but that is ultimately the solution. If they do mention something which you believe is the solution, get excited about that option. Immediately provide positive feedback for them giving you the right answer. This is the reaction they are looking for and hoping for. It's the same with children, positive feedback for actions they take out of choice is far more effective than negative feedback. The possibility of reward and seeing approval in people is a fantastic way to get people to see your point of view.

If however, the customer doesn't suggest any ideas which are suitable, start to make a few suggestions of your own. You can paraphrase them with things like "what we tried in the past ..." or "what I've seen work ...". For example if they never suggest creating recurring revenue, you could say "in order to solve your cash flow problem, I have seen creating a recurring revenue product work in the past". After you've made a few suggestions, ask the customer what they think the priority solution would be. Ideally, they'll choose your solution and what you suggested. If they are adamant that traffic or social media marketing will solve their problem, now is the time to gently use your expert status to guide them to what will work. Interestingly, the way to get them there is to actually agree with them.

Let's say you want them to suggest that creating a recurring revenue product is the best solution but they are insistent on social media marketing. Most funnel builders and marketing experts will immediately disagree with the customer, tell them they're wrong, and then tell them a horror story about why it wouldn't work. Another significant percentage of funnel builders will agree with the customer, do the social media marketing, and wonder why the customer has fired them when it hasn't got them results. If you're adamant that creating a recurring revenue product is right for the customer, but they suggest social media marketing, you need to agree with them first, then tell them how we can get there. For example:

"Mr. Customer I completely agree that social media marketing will take your business to the next level. I want to make sure that we can get there and utilise any social activities as best we can. My only concern is that without something like a recurring revenue product we will just get ourselves into the same situation. I agree that we need to do social media marketing and I agree that at some point it will be a priority. However right now, without a recurring revenue product, our social media marketing might go to waste. Does that sound logical?"

Asking "does that sound logical?" It's a hypothetical question of course. No one wants to seem illogical, so of course they'll agree with you. You're also not telling them that it's a bad idea, you're just suggesting that it's not the right time. I think it's fantastic that you want to run a marathon, but you should probably run a 10k first. I think it's fantastic that you want to buy a car, shall we get you your driving licence first? Agreeing with the customer shows them that you are on the same side. It's usually during these kinds of conversations that customers believe they are on the opposing side to the consultant. Consultants are desperate to be seen as right, customers are desperate to be seen as in control. Remember, you're on the same side of the table. You both want what's best for the customer. Telling them they are wrong and that it's a bad idea it isn't going to help the situation.

Finding something to agree with is a hundred times more effective. Now you've arrived at a solution that you can give advice on and focused on one priority, you are going to do everything you can to help them with that one solution. Now is another good time to repeat back what you talked about.

You: So Mr. Customer, you told me that you want to sell the business in five years but you need to sort out inconsistent cash flow. You told me that you think creating a recurring revenue product is the priority. Is that right?

Customer: Yes

You: Fantastic, would you like some help with that?-Or-would you like me to take you through that?

The customer of course is going to want you to take them through that specific process and now as far as they're concerned it's their idea. That means they are going to be far more receptive and open to what you're selling them. They've told you everything and now this is their idea. They are 100% on board with anything you tell them. Stop by this point, you've probably got about half an hour worth of call left. You will want to go through a high level process and the steps on the solution. No need to go into too much depth, because you're going to ask them if they would like a secondary piece of content. The proposal.

Mr. Customer, in terms of creating recurring revenue we have a process whereby we identify your top clients, reach out to them, understand what they would buy every single month, create a payment processor which takes subscription payments and deliver a monthly product. Would you like me to send you an in-depth proposal outlining our solution?

The customer by this point is eager for you to take over their idea and give your best thoughts. This is now when you can send a proposal, and the customer has essentially bought the solution already. The proposal is merely a formality.

The growth session is probably the most complex and malleable part of the process. If you've just read that section and you're now thinking "holy ship, there's so much to take in here", please don't worry. This is after years of consulting myself. And I can assure you, that I was terrible at it for most of that time. Every week I personally am getting better at consulting. My advice is to remember three core components to offering growth sessions:

1. Stay quiet and give yourself and your customer time to think. This takes the pressure off having to have the right answer immediately all the time.
2. Let the customer tell you what they'll buy, stop trying to sell them a solution.
3. You're perfectly entitled to ask questions, no one expects you to give free advice.

In truth, this script really just runs on a bit of a loop. It's actually just the same handful of questions asked over and over and over; we just record the answers. Have you ever worked with a consultant where they ask you a ton of questions, and then repeating back one sentence gives you absolute clarity? It feels amazing when someone hands that back to you; it's like distilling down gallons of water into delicious smoky whiskey. It sometimes takes someone else to sift through all of your thoughts and information, in order to come back with a succinct idea.

All you are doing at the start is asking about their goals, why they're important and what the priorities. You are also asking about their problems, why that's a problem, and what's the priority. By asking them to describe their day, you understand where they are. You repeat back to them their priority goal, priority problem and ask them if they'd like help.

Don't overcomplicate it. My advice would also be to find someone in the Sell Your Service Facebook group[5] and ask if they'd like to practice running a growth session with you. After they've agreed to seeing a proposal from you, we now need to send one.

---

[5] sellyourservice.co.uk/facebook

Proposal

For some reason, proposals have become the bane of many funnel builders, marketing agencies and freelancers. There is a misconception that they're difficult to write, take ages and if the customer hates it, they won't bite.

1. Your proposals should take 30 minutes to write, tops.
2. You should write the proposal immediately after offering it to the client (don't procrastinate).
3. A short, badly written proposal will still convert the right customer. You can't lose a sale because of one thing.

The fear of course is that we write up the proposal, and if we do a bad job, the customer will turn around and say "I'm not interested". We also see proposals from competitors, other industries, online and in movies, beautifully put together, expertly designed - elaborate documents themselves worthy of praise.

I however, along with my business partners, have written six and seven figure proposals using nothing but Microsoft Word. It's been approximately 6 to 8 pages long and includes almost no design work. The rule of thumb is that a badly written proposal to the right customer will always convert better than a beautifully designed proposal to the wrong customer.

It's a bit like advertising. A mediocre advert with the right message to the right customer will convert a hundred times better than a beautifully stunning advert to the wrong audience. I'm reminded of a joke where a stand-up comedian was doing an 'out of retirement tour' across the United States. He was very high-profile and people were eager to see him back in action. What made it more extraordinary was that he was playing smaller gigs and venues, going back to his roots. In one gig in New York City, he stood up on stage, delivered his opening joke, and not one single person laughed. He went through his entire set and barely got a chuckle out of the audience. He came off stage called up his Manager immediately and said "I'm quitting the game, it's clear I lost it. Maybe I never had it?" After walking past the bar, the manager tapped him on the shoulder and asked him "what the hell was that?" The comedian turned around shocked, looked at the manager and said "Yes I know! My material sucked!". The manager replied "no, they told me that you spoke fluent Italian. This is an Italian tour group, they couldn't understand a word you were saying." Know your audience!

The reason I believe proposals should be easy to write is because the customer has told you what they want to buy. During the growth session (which is why these are so important) they have told their priorities, the solution they want, the problems they're solving and the future they want.

It's another way of saying "the future that they want" is full of benefits. Your proposal should essentially be a list of benefits that the customer is going to experience after handing you some money. If you had a standard word document delivered to the customer, that was short, easy to read and demonstrated that you not only listened but you agree with them and understood their situation, then you've got yourself a sale.

The truth is that most customers are ready to buy if they've asked for a proposal. Proposals are a formality. This is the close. You have already *sold* the project or marketing funnel to them. They've already bought it. Now you just need to close them.

As I mentioned, the second you get off that call, or leave that meeting, start writing the proposal. We use BetterProposals.io for all our proposals. I've even got a marketing funnel template inside there that you can find.

The proposal is read in this order, by the customer:
1. Cover letter
2. Costs/Investment
3. Timescale
4. Solution
5. Case study
6. Goals
7. Where are we now?
8. Next steps

The proposal is delivered in this order, by you:
1. Cover letter
2. Goals
3. Where are we now?
4. Solution
5. Case study
6. Investment
7. Timescale
8. Next steps

The proposal is written, by you, in this order:
1. Next steps
2. Investment
3. Timescale
4. Solution
5. Where are we now?
6. Goals
7. Case study
8. Cover letter

As you can see, all three orders are different. While the document is presented in a logical order, it's read by the customer in a different order. And you're going to write it in 1/3rd of the time it usually takes you, maybe even faster.

Each proposal you write should get faster each time. Not only because you'll get better at it, but the more you specialise in what you do, the less you'll need to edit the content of the proposal. Other than the customer's name and goals, many of the solutions and benefits are going to be identical for each project.

If you want to download a proposal template head to sellyourservice.co.uk/fivefigurefunnels and you can get a blank marketing funnel proposal to use with your customers. Also, remember that there is a marketing funnel proposal at betterproposals.io written by me. Both are the same.

I'll explain each stage in the order that I'd write a proposal from scratch. Then, you'll reuse many aspects of the proposal for each new customer and project - massively increasing your productivity and speed of delivery.

Next steps

I've read so many proposals, sales letters and pitch decks that fail to include a clear next steps section that it's a wonder anyone makes any sales at all. Without question, the most important page in the whole document is a clear and specific instruction as to what the customer must do next, in order to move ahead and start solving their problems.

You cannot be too obvious or clear in this section. Forget feeling patronising or like it's too obvious. You literally need to spell out what the reader must do, if they want to start working with you. So many funnel builders believe that either the customer will know what to do, or that *telling* them what to do is pressuring them. Remember, if you're at the proposal stage, they've already bought. They've made the decision internally to buy from you and they want to work with you. The proposal is a formality. But you must know what you want the customer to do.

Don't wait for them to ask "so what happens now?" or "what do we need to do?" You need to tell them. You must create a single specific page that explicitly tells them what they must do and say in order to start working with you. Start by making a list of what you need:

- 50% deposit
- Signed terms of engagement (contract)
- Content up front

One of the reasons I love BetterProposals.io is because they have a digital signature section that allows readers to sign *and* then redirects them to a page where they can pay via credit card.

Do you have a payment page?

Rule #1 of selling is make it easy to take the customer's money. If you're still relying on bank transfers, cheques and wiring money from different accounts you're making it hard to take the customers cash. Create a page like sellyourservice.co.uk/balance where customers can pay deposits, clear balances owed and easily pay you for your services.

We ALWAYS get a signature accepting the proposal and any terms (if needed). I will not, ever, move forward on a project unless I have a signature. It's too easy to move the goal posts later on.

Finally, and this is something seriously worth considering, get the content from the customer up front. You cannot do most of the work of a marketing funnel builder without content. If you're the one creating the content, then fine, make sure that they have their first content session booked in. But one of the biggest mistakes I made was to start working on projects with zero content from the customer and then wait months (years even) for content to come later. If they don't have the content, then offer to work on it with them (for a price of course).

You'll want to word the page something like the below.

Next steps
You're going to love working with us and we're going to get [customer business name] epic results.
Sign below to confirm that this is the right solution for you.
We require a 50% deposit.
Once we've received payment, a signed contract and you've booked your first session/received your content, we'll start working.
Make sure you click below to sign and send over the deposit to secure your place.

Investment

It's the investment page, not the pricing page. They're investing in their business, not giving you money. So how much do they need to invest?

My advice is keep this simple. Like, super simple. The less detail the better. Be up front with your costs and never ever second guess your prices. You know what you need to charge. Don't let the numbers scare or fool you. Write out each line item and a cost. Use a total cost at the bottom and separate monthly and one off costs.

Include tax if you need to. No need to go into too much detail. I used to make the mistake of writing out detailed bullet points and descriptions for each line item. Instead now I just refer to the stage of the project, a brief description and a price.

Use something like the below.

Investment
One off investment

Marketing audit Review of website, traffic and current set up to identify opportunities and areas to improve	£4500
Product workshop Creation of new products to sell to customers to increase revenue per customer and customer value	£4500
Content and branding Building benefits for each product to use for marketing and sales collateral	£4000
Email automation Subscriber follow up and nurture and sales automation for new and old products	£7500
Launch campaign Sell new products to market	£3500
One off total	£25,000

Continued required work

Refuel process Continuing clean up of spam data and updating subscribers to reduce cost per sale	£750 pm
Monthly total	£750 pm

Suggested enhancements
The above necessary requirements are what we believe the project requires
to achieve its minimum goals. The below are additional enhancements that
we believe will accelerate the path to our goals.

Audience to sale automation 3 stage process to convert visitors and traffic into sales with zero external input	£5000
Low hanging fruit sales identification Target potential leads and sales that should have bought but haven't and identify both number and location	£2500
Targeted advertising campaign Continued traffic to specific landing pages to convert into sales	£2500 pm

After writing a few proposals, you should be reusing your investment page
over and over. If you're not, it's a sign that you're not focused enough on
your offering and you're customising each project per customer.

Timescale

Partnerships work when above all else, each side knows when things are
happening. Of the 3 core aspects of a successful partnership (timescale,
objectives and values), timescales is what people get most stuck on.

You need to tell your customers when you'll complete each stage. And
YOU must tell them when you need their input. I once had a customer
relationship break down in a matter of hours when my expectations of
timescale didn't match theirs. In this particular case, they had taken months
to get any content or feedback to me. They eventually sent responses but it
was too late and I had booked other projects. I told them that I'm not a drive-
thru, I have deadlines to adhere to and so do they. Needless to say, the project
dissolved and we parted ways. If you're serious about running a funnel
business, you need to make sure that you hold customers to objectives too.

Again, keep it simple. Don't give dates, give time scales. We can give dates
during project management. Just tell them that it takes 4 weeks to write an
email campaign *assuming* they can get you everything they need.

Customers aren't disappointed when they don't set goals. They're
disappointed when goals take longer than stated. It's critical that we set
realistic timescales from the start. Hold them accountable as you will yourself.
The timescales is usually the most important part that the customer is signing
when they agree and close.

We're eager to start!

How often have you heard this one? "It won't be a problem to get work from us Mike, we're ready to go!" Every single customer I've ever worked with has said this and every single time, they have been the hold up. Content, images, workshop dates, payments, access, you name it. I'm super clear about my deadlines and as a rule I 4X everything that I set a time to. As a rule, it'll take 4X longer than I think. So I make that adjustment and if the customer recoils and says "4 weeks for a landing page?!" I'll gladly respond and say "that's the average time. If we get a move on it can be much much shorter." Without fail, almost every time, it's either 4 weeks. At worst, it'll be on time, at best, it'll be earlier and we're ahead of schedule.

Solution

This is where most funnel builders get confused and over complicate things. The most common question I have from funnel builders about the solution section is "my customers just want to know what they're buying."

The fallacy is believing that this means they want to see the features and 'nuts and bolts' of what they're buying and in truth, they really, really do not. It doesn't serve anyone to start going into technical detail about what you and your team are going to build, no matter how tempting it is to get this down on paper.

You should have already written out 'The Solution'. It's basically the milestones and steps in chapter 3, Assets. You've got milestones, you've got steps and you've got benefits. During your sales calls and meetings you've gone over the model. You've talked about the steps that you'd recommend and talked about how you can help. You've also got benefits to what you do and *those* are what customers want to read.

Check out these two solutions for a financial services business below:

Solution 1.
Investment and saving strategy
- 15 point audit of your finances and records to determine the best course for investment.
- Monthly and weekly budget analysing what costs can be cut.
- Strategic choice of investment plans and saving options in a report.

Solution 2.

Have more fun saving (and do it while you sleep)

- Custom tailored plan to see exactly how much money you'll make.
- Spending plan and painless 'save while you sleep' plan.
- Confidently know your money is in the best place (and you can move it any time).

These two solutions are for the exact same financial service. Not even a complex one. Arguably, your bank should be providing this. However, the trap that people fall into is thinking that they need to make the solution sound more professional and use words like strategic, tactical and integrated.

Really, this just turns the customer off. Why? Because a solution isn't about you or the service, it's about *them*. A benefit is a better future that the customer can imagine. No one cares about a 15 point audit. If anything, that sounds awful. Instead, what does a customer want to see or experience in their future? Would you rather have an audit in the near future, or a plan to see how much money you'll make?

Both are the same solution but one is sold as a feature and the other is sold as a future. Sell futures, not features.

Where are we now? (problem, goals, resources)

We're now going to include a problems, goals and current resources page, but we call it .Where are we now?' It's an overview of what the customer has told us about their business and the situation they're in. There are three key parts to this section:

1. Outline the problems faced in the business.
2. Repeat back the top 5 goals of the customer.
3. Cover the resources/current position they're in.

I also like to include a section called 'If we don't act now' which acts as a way of showing why they need to do this sooner rather than later.

There's an example below, but don't over complicate it. You are repeating back what the customer has told *you* during the discovery and consultation stage. It honestly is as simple as that. Don't mince words or try to embellish what they've said. Use their language and their words. Use their goals and their interpretation of the situation.

We're going to help [customer name] get [result].

Where we are now

[Customer name] is talking to [your business name] because they want to achieve [goal].

[Customer name] is a [business type]. Currently they are [experiencing problem] where they need to achieve [goal] instead.

At the moment, [customer name] are in the following situation:

- [Roadblocks preventing goal E.g. no ecommerce store]
- [Roadblocks preventing goal E.g. no ecommerce store]
- [Roadblocks preventing goal E.g. no ecommerce store]
- [Roadblocks preventing goal E.g. no ecommerce store]
- [Roadblocks preventing goal E.g. no ecommerce store]

If we don't act now

Because [change/opportunity/threat technology], this means [result]

Because [change/opportunity/threat sociological], this means [result]

Because [change/opportunity/threat economic], this means [result]

What are we working with?

- [Current situation bullet points E.g. traffic, leads, customers etc.]
- [Current situation bullet points E.g. traffic, leads, customers etc.]
- [Current situation bullet points E.g. traffic, leads, customers etc.]
- [Current situation bullet points E.g. traffic, leads, customers etc.]
- [Current situation bullet points E.g. traffic, leads, customers etc.]

If [customer name] can just solve [roadblock], they'd be able to achieve [goal] which would let them [benefit].

Where we want to be

[Customer name] wants to achieve [goal]. With that, they'll [benefit] and [results].

[Customer name] also wants to [solve problem or achieve goal] and [solve problem or achieve goal].

- [Bullet point list goals E.g. 10 000 visitors per year]
- [Bullet point list goals E.g. 10 000 visitors per year]
- [Bullet point list goals E.g. 10 000 visitors per year]
- [Bullet point list goals E.g. 10 000 visitors per year]
- [Bullet point list goals E.g. 10 000 visitors per year]

I've got an example of the types of language we use below, following the exact same process of just replacing the goals and problems with what the customer has told us.

XXX is talking to Sell Your Service because they want to grow revenue with a repeatable sales process.

XXX is a translation company in the process of a buyout. Currently, they are looking to grow sales and create a repeatable sales process so they can strengthen their seller position.

At the moment, XXX are in the following situation:

No defined sales process for attracting new clients and business.

No referral process for current customers.

0% spent on marketing, sales and acquisition.

IF WE DON'T ACT NOW...

Because XXX is in the process of being bought, this means XXX is in a stronger position if there is growth in sales.

Because nothing is certain, this means XXX can mitigate risk with a repeatable sales process that attracts and converts customers.

As the business grows anyway, XXX needs a sales process that they can hire with and use for scaling their business

WHAT ARE WE WORKING WITH?

£650 000 per year in revenue.

Growing roughly 20% year on year.

Around 30 current customers of varying value.

No lead generation process.

No account management.

"If XXX can create a repeatable sales process, they'd be able to grow revenue and sales which would help them mitigate risk and strengthen their seller position in a buy out."

WHERE WE WANT TO BE

XXX wants to create a sales process and drive new sales within a year. With that, they'll strengthen their position in a buyout and mitigate risk if there is no sale.

XXX also wants to hire a sales/account role and provide both training and sales resources to maximise return on a hire.

£200 000 revenue goal from new sales within a year.

More big ticket clients at £80 000+ per customer.

Repeatable sales process to attract new customers.

Account management process to drive new sales from previous customers.

Push to over £1m in revenue in 2019.

If you repeat back to a customer everything they've told you, it shows that you've listened and you're paying attention. Customers will also tell you what they want to buy. So if you just write up everything they've told you, *they* are writing the sales part of the proposal.

Case Study

I'm going to show you the easiest method IN THE WORLD to increase your marketing funnel project proposal conversion rates.

When we submit a marketing funnel project proposal to a customer, it's in their hands whether they buy. That's it, that's all you can do.

It's like walking out of an exam. You've submitted your answers. Nothing else you can do but wait and pray (and in my case disappear for a few months and pick them up late after coming home from travelling).

So how can we increase the likelihood that someone will sign up to a marketing funnel project?

Case studies aren't long

The biggest roadblock people see when thinking about creating case studies, is how lengthy they are. We're used to seeing huge, long reams of paper reports called 'A Case Study'. Case studies aren't long or even complex. They're just designed to tell a story about someone who experienced the same thing as your customers. If you want to sell more marketing funnels, get a few case studies under your belt.

Isn't a case study basically a portfolio piece?

Not exactly. Case studies can be written about your customers and projects of course. But you can do case studies on other businesses. As long as you are crystal clear that it's a report and not a portfolio piece, you can write up how another business achieved a goal with similar results.

Pro tip: whip out your proposal from previous projects to write SUPER FAST case studies. You'll see why in a bit. You can either write these up as individual web pages or as a document to include with your proposals. You're only going to write a few at a time and you'll keep them. So stack a few up and keep them handy.

This is how…

Case studies start like any other piece of content. Using headlines.

'This is how…' is one of the most powerful and popular headlines for B2B content according to BuzzSumo.

This is what [customer name] did to [get result]

This is what APAC did to keep more course members.

This is what CKS did to sell courses online.

This is what WPE did to increase revenue from their email list.

We want to use the same results and language that your new customer wants.

Problem faced

What was the problem that your previous customer faced? What was it about their business that another business will recognise?

We recognise aspirational phrases (this is how…) and then we recognise our own situation through a problem.

[customer name] suffered from [problem].

They wanted to [reach goal] and [have result]. But their [problem] meant it was hard to [repeat result].

APAC had no online sales or platform to deliver online courses.

They wanted to have 50% of revenue come from online course sales. But having no online platform meant it was impossible to generate revenue online from selling courses.

Repeating results and problems looks a little weird on paper, when written down. But as long as you make it sound like a human wrote it, it's a very powerful tactic.

Change faced

So why are they addressing this now? Why is this important or worth looking at today? There are threats and there are opportunities in the world. We have to show why our previous customer worked to move NOW and what they faced. It's also good if you can use the same threats/opportunities that your current customers are facing.

When [technology change] it meant that [change in result]. We can use any kind of chance. Technological, economic or sociological. Something within those areas that changes and presents a threat or opportunity. When their courses became so popular, it meant that they had to turn down customers and lost focus on finding new customers because they were delivering in person. Show what's happening that they need to address. Not just the problems, but things that are changing outside of their control.

Knife twist

After the 'change faced' section, I like to top that with a knife twist. We basically finish the sentence – And on top of all that... I'll research another problem or roadblock which is preventing them from achieving their goals. On top of that, APAC needed to give time back to the owners and management (who were delivering the courses) so they could focus on running the business. This finishes the problem section (notice how short it is) and we can move onto the solution part.

What they had

These sections are bullet points. We'll introduce what the previous customer had before working with us. Where they started. Traffic, leads, customers, revenue etc. We just list out the top 3 items which are relevant to the marketing funnel proposal. Usually leads, sales, traffic.

When we first met APAC they had:
- A list of over 5000 who had never bought online.
- No online delivery method.
- No recurring sales from online revenue.

What they have

Then we explore what they've got now. What we helped them get. Same process of introducing the bullet points and using the top 3 results they now have. Pro tip: Use the same bullet points from above and do a before/after comparison for extra impact.

Now APAC has:
- Over 2000 monthly subscribers to their online course.
- Fully functioning LMS system with online course delivery and payment systems.
- £20 000 a month revenue from recurring online sales.

Solution built

We're going to show the solution that we built for the previous customer. Again, it's not massively detailed, but it's a highlight of what they're getting. If you can use the exact same language as your new customer E.g. LMS or funnel etc. you'll score well.

We built our LMS funnel for them which included:
- Sales automation to increase conversions.
- Easy content management for new courses.
- Online reporting for delivery and consumption.

Benefits

We're starting to wrap up the case study, and to finish we're going to show how our customer's life is better. Benefits are how your LIFE is better. Results are measurable differences. Features, believe it or not are vital to a proposal too. That's the solution.

APAC now has/sees:
- More people buying with lower expenses.
- Time back to management and not on delivery.
- Increased online revenue with higher margins.

Social proof

Finally, we like to wrap up the proposal with social proof. This will either be a testimonial quote or a screenshot of a result. For example, a traffic increase or increase in email subscribers would be worth showing a screenshot of.

So there we have it. If you want to increase your marketing funnel proposal close rates, use case studies. Include a headline introducing what you're going to show them. Then move on to the problems faced and changes happening that they need to address. Work through what they had and what you did to solve it. Show what they have now and present this to your customers. Include case studies in your proposals and see how they improve conversion rates. They're also awesome to send over to customers as a talking point.

Cover letter

Finally, I believe that adding a short punchy cover letter is a great way to start a proposal. People do read them and for the sake of using a template like the below, it can really push you apart from other submissions.

Cover letters are not the entire proposal, they're also not justifications for the price or a place to get excuses out of the way. A cover letter is designed to thank the customer, highlight the core solution and ask for feedback. Something like the below:

Dear Ann

I wanted to thank you for the opportunity to present this strategy and proposal to XXX.

I've taken on board everything that we've gone over, including your goals and current numbers and I've put together a solution that meets the needs of your growth.

Sell Your Service has built sales and acquisition strategies that help service business attract more paying clients and scale their sales efforts.

I know that XXX can benefit from this plan too.

Customer and lead generation plan.

Sales gameplan for long term sales success.

Account manager and hiring strategy.

I'm constantly looking to improve the way I deal with customers. If there is any feedback you have, it's seriously important to me and I'd gladly welcome questions or comments.

I'm extremely excited to partner with XXX and I can't wait to see how quickly we can grow your revenue.

Sincerely

[signature]

Michael Killen

Sell Your Service

Presenting

I don't believe that success is the result of one action or magic turning point. But if I had to pinpoint the action that gave the largest significant impact on my sales and funnel business, it's refusing to hand the proposal over until we've presented it live.

One of the reasons it's so critical to get the proposal written quickly, is because you want to get on a call or book a meeting with the customer. If you're really serious about getting these sales in and closed, book the call before you finish the presentation. That way you'll force yourself to write up the proposal fast.

Getting on a call also allows you the highest chance of closing the deal. Believe it or not, a customer is *most* likely to buy as soon as you've finished the presentation. All the objections and complaints about pricing or being given time to think it over are just excuses.

You are far more likely to close a deal after a call because that's when the customer's interest is at its peak. They're never going to be more hot to the idea and project than they are now. It's time to capitalise on that.

Here's the basic order you'll follow to get on a call:

1. Finish your discovery meeting.
2. Write the proposal THAT DAY (yes - immediately after the call while it's fresh).
3. Book a call/meeting with them within a week of your previous call (this is why you might want to book the call at the end of the meeting in case they're away or busy).
4. Tell them you have almost finished the presentation but that you want to check a few things before you present to them.
5. Get on a call and run through the proposal.
6. Close them at the end of the call.

Booking the presentation call

At the end of your discovery meeting, before you've written the proposal, you need to finish the meeting with something like the below.

"Hey Miss Customer, I want to make sure I get a proposal in front of you as quickly as possible. Are you free next Tuesday for me to show you what we can do?"

Get a time and a date and get a firm commitment. The faster you move through the process, the more likely the customer is to buy. There is a massive difference between desperate and hungry. Desperation is unattractive and customers can smell it a mile off. Hungry means you're ready to go and you want to work with them. Hungry means you're determined to make a difference. Show them you're hungry.

If you've left the meeting or you're doing this via Zoom calls or Skype, then book a presentation that way and make sure you can share your screen. Occasionally, I've had to leave the meeting without a commitment on the next meeting. It does happen and we can still get on track. I like to use an email like the below.

"Hey Miss Customer. I've almost completed the proposal and I wanted to run through it with you and ask you a few more questions before sending the final version that you'd be happy with. Are you free next Tuesday at 3pm? Or I can do Wednesday at 11am or 2pm?"

The reason I don't tell them it's complete is because they'll want the price and to see the cost. I want to make sure that I control the narrative of the proposal and offer before they jump to conclusions about cost. If they ask you to send over the proposal, agree with them but don't yield (a technique you'll see a lot later).

"Hey Miss Customer, I'll send over the proposal no problem. I just have a couple more questions to ask before I send the final version. Your time is too valuable to go back and forth over a document that we could just read once."

On the call

Presenting a proposal to a customer could also be called pitching. Don't worry about slick presentation styles and fast talking sales pitches of the past. We're going to let the customer know what's wrong with their business, repeat back what they've told us and tell them how to fix it. Like most things, practice is absolutely paramount. But don't worry about getting it 'perfect', you're going to do just fine reading off the proposal. There's a bizarre fetish in entrepreneur circles that we should sell without selling, or that 'pitching' is bad and customers hate it. It's a bit like saying that you hated vegetables as a kid and now you're sticking to that conclusion. Pitching is one of the BIGGEST benefits that you can offer a customer. When done well, they don't just respond positively to you or even buy from you, they'll *thank* you for presenting the solution in a clear, straightforward manner.

As someone who has pitched for work hundreds (maybe even thousands) of times, and someone who has seen hundreds of pitches, there is a clear difference between a great pitch and a bad one. I'm going to show you what I do, on a call, to close a deal and have a customer *thank you* for pitching and presenting to them.

Good pitch

- Focuses on the customer.
- Repeats back what the customer has told us.
- Makes it clear what the next steps are.
- Gets the customer to sign up because they're excited.
- Demonstrates that you're enthusiastic about the solution.

Bad pitch

- Focuses on you or the product.
- Uses over complicated language to appear more technical.
- Acts as educational content rather than actionable.
- Tells the customer what you think they want rather than demonstrating that you've listened.
- Is delivered unemotionally with technical language and cold delivery.

What if they don't turn up, cancel, or are late?

I remember a few years back one of Liv's friend's husband asked to talk to me. I was very excited about the opportunity as he ran a large company responsible for manufacturing video game components. I thought this could be a huge opportunity for me.

He however, obviously thought the same thing - that he was offering me a chance or that I was very lucky to talk to him. Waiting in his reception area, I was told he'd be "just a minute" and then it was "just another ten minutes." It was already 10 minutes into our meeting and he was late. I had two choices.

Either wait and out of politeness understand that he's a busy man and I could talk to him. Or, I could offer to rearrange the meeting. As a rule, I set 45 minute meetings. I tell people as soon as I've booked a meeting that I've got a call straight after so I can't fuck around talking about Game Of Thrones.

It's at this point we're either desperate or hungry. Desperate people wait. Hungry people hunt. When his assistant walked over to me a 3rd time, she started explaining he's stuck in a meeting and he'll just be a few more minutes. "No problem" I replied "Let's rebook. I have another call I need to make." I was pulling away and demonstrating that I was hungry, not desperate. The assistant looked stunned. "He'll really be here in a minute!" she proclaimed, which might have been true, but I didn't see him anywhere and the coffee wasn't good enough to hang around. "Honestly it's no problem. I'll head out and Kev can rebook" I said with a huge smile. Accepting defeat with grace and a smile is good sportsmanship. Leaving before the call and valuing your time enough to go hunting elsewhere, with that same huge smile while you leave, is far more powerful.

Before I had even reached the door, Kev miraculously disappeared. The fear of offense had transferred from me, leaving, to him, ignoring me. Funny how quickly an important meeting can be exited when you're walking out the door.

Of course deep down, I was shaking and nervous. I thought I'd look like an absolute wanker. Who leaves like that!? People who are busy and know when something is not worth their time, that's who. Plus, you know that deep down during the meeting, you don't feel valued. It's not a nice start to a relationship and I'm a firm believer of starting as you mean to go on. Sure enough Kev did sit down with me in the end, and while the relationship never went anywhere anyway, it was a valuable lesson that if you don't value your time, no one else will.

Any pitch you make should result in one thing: moving the customer to the next stage. That's all. The next stage in this example is...

And that's where most pitches and calls break down. The funnel builder themselves doesn't even know what they're pitching for! Just like with the Next Steps section of the proposal, you have to be 100% on what you're asking for. Be specific. You're not asking them to "buy", that's not clear enough. What you're asking for is a 50% deposit and a signed contract. Literally, you need to be able to say "in order for us to go ahead, we need a 50% deposit and a signature here" pointing to the dotted line. The clearer you are on the call to action and next step, the easier the call.

On the call, or during the live presentation, bring up each page of the proposal just as we wrote it earlier. As a rule, too much text or just a wall of words on a screen isn't compelling or engaging which is why our sections in our proposals are short, focused on bullet points and not wordy.

Follow the outline that you deliver the proposal in the same order.

1. Cover letter
2. Goals
3. Where are we now?
4. Solution
5. Case study
6. Investment
7. Timescale
8. Next steps

Keep it conversational and spend 5 minutes per section. No need to get overly complex. If you're comfortable presenting, my advice would be to refer back to earlier meetings and use phrases like "during our call you told us..." and "I distinctly remember you telling me..." Make sure it's clear that you're focused on them and their business, their lives.

Go through the pitch and at the end of each section E.g. goals, where are we now etc. ask the customer "have I understood that correctly?" And listen to their feedback. Chances are, if you've done your job, they'll say "yes, you've understood that."

I don't like to ask "does that make sense?" or "do you understand that?" I make the assumption that the customer is smart and can understand me. Also, when someone doesn't understand, it's easier to put the onerous on yourself asking if you've understood them. After running through the pitch, we want to finish on the Next Steps section and tell them what they need to do to start working with us. This is more commonly called 'Closing'.

Assume the sale

Before we get into the practice and methods of closing, as with most things, your mindset will play the biggest role here in determining whether people will buy from you. And your mindset at this stage (in fact during the entire call) needs to be 'assume the sale'. What I mean by this, is that you must assume that the customer wants to buy from you. Assume that if they're looking at the proposal with you, it means they want to buy. People don't listen to pitches and read proposals because they're bored. They do it because they want to buy.

What do you think the #1 most common reason is that the customer doesn't buy? It's not price, it's not competitors or a USP. It isn't your portfolio or logo or brand. The number 1 reason that most businesses don't buy is because they're never *asked* to buy. That's right. The most common reason for a sale to fall through is because the sales person never asks the customer "do we have your business?" Isn't that insane? I've lost count of the number of sales calls I've been in, listened into and had given to me where the sales person never once asks "do you want to buy?"

So many pitches and presentations talk around the close, offering other, weaker endings to the end of a pitch.

- So does anyone have any questions?
- Thank you for listening
- We'll wait to hear from you

The absolute #1 objective for you is to ask the customer "do you want to buy the thing I've just sold to you?" Ideally, the customer says yes. Second best is they say no. Worst of all is never asking.

If we assume that the customer wants to buy, *asking* them if they want to buy is a no brainer. Imagine how easy life would be if you could just ask people if they do/don't want something and then just delivering it. Bliss. You're not giving your customers the chance to make life easy for you.

Don't ever assume that the customer is going to ask if they can buy from you. This is a massive mistake that all business owners and sales people make at some point. They assume that if their customer wants it badly enough, they'll ask if they can buy. If you think that asking the customer for the sale is embarrassing or uncomfortable (which I admit it can be), imagine how the customer feels asking if they can buy? For all you know, they're eager to buy but you're just not offering them the chance.

Finish the presentation with a close, which is to say, tell the customer what the next step is and ask them if they want to do that next step.

"Mrs Customer, we can get started today, we just need a signature and a deposit. Can I get a signature here?"

Or "Mr. Customer, we can get started on this right away. We just need a deposit and a signature. How would you like to pay?"

Here's the tricky part though. You're *looking* for a rejection. You want someone to say "no" or "not yet". The sale comes *after* the objection. You want the customer to object and tell you why they can't buy right now.

Of course, some of the time, the customer will say "awesome, we'll pay by card. Let's go!" It does happen. But not all the time. And a customer giving an objection isn't them saying no forever, it's them saying "not until…"

"We're not sure we need all 5 landing pages."

"Is there any way we can get this finished in July, 3 months sooner than the plan?"

"What about chatbots? Do we need them? Could we replace this with a chatbot?"

Listening to the reasons they don't want to buy, listening to their objections, is a critical part of the sales process and building a relationship. Remember, assume the sale, assume the customer wants to buy. But they feel they need to get clarity on the timeline or needs or project. If anything, them giving you an objection is them asking you "I want to buy this, help me justify it in my mind."

Turning an objection is simple. Don't over complicate it. ARC. Agree Remind/Reason Close. That's as complex as it needs to get. Agree, Remind/Reason, Close.

"Mr. Customer you're absolutely right. We could replace the entire system with a chatbot. And I think at some point we'll talk about adding that in. One of the reasons we decided against the chatbot right now was because of your need for new sales copy. We can get started on this right now with a signed contract and deposit."

What I did was agree - *Mr. Customer you're absolutely right. We could replace the entire system with a chatbot.* Making the customer feel acknowledged and listened to. We're on the same side of the table. You're on their side! Don't disagree with them. They're not challenging you, they're looking for logical justifications to tell other people when they're asked the same question.

We reminded him - *One of the reasons we decided against the chatbot right now was because of your need for new sales copy.* Reinforcing our early reasons for choosing that path. Notice how before that, we also said that we're open to adding chatbots? No problem at all - agree!

We closed - *We can get started on this right now with a signed contract and deposit.* We told him the next steps and reminded him of what we need to do next.

Agree with the customer, remind them or give reason, close. ARC.

But what if they tell you it's too expensive?

The problem is that a lot of the time when customers are going through the closing process with us, and we say to the customer "okay this is going to be £25000 or £100 000" or whatever the price is and they'll say "oh wow that's pretty expensive".

A lot of sales coaches are going to tell you that's an objection. It's not.

Saying it's too expensive or saying they can't afford the product, or they don't have the money is not an objection. Here's what most sales coaches will teach you. They'll teach you that someone saying "that's expensive" or they "can't afford that" is an objection and you need to turn that objection. The easiest way we know to turn an objection, are things like feel, felt, found.

"Hey I totally understand how you feel. A lot of customers felt the same way. And what we found is that the value we're going to deliver through this final project is going to outpace that £25000 initial investment hundreds and hundreds of times".

Feel, felt, found - which by the way is still a fantastic method of turning other objections like the earlier ones.

But it's not an objection saying something is too expensive. Saying that they haven't got the money is not an objection. It's a problem. The customer saying "this is expensive" is their problem. That's a framework in their state of mind that they perceive your product as expensive compared to their situation.

It's not expensive, but customers are still going to say to you "wow this seems expensive. That's a lot of money" and the way that I get around that, is I agree with them. Then I tell them to sign and send a deposit.

When a customer says to me "Well that's a lot of money that's pretty expensive. I don't know if we've got that in the account right now." I'll reply with "I totally agree man it is expensive. What isn't nowadays? Sign this and send us a deposit."

That's the way that you want to start framing this particular problem. It's not an objection from your customers. An objection is when they say "okay well how is it that we're going to be able to convert followers from Facebook, into leads?"

Until they understand that process, that's an objection. That's a valid objection of something that you haven't covered. You could be the best salesperson in the world, deliver the most comprehensive in-depth value driven pitch ever, and the customer could still turn around to you and say "this doesn't seem like it's worth it. I don't know if we've got this kind of money".

That's their problem. Money is their problem. Their money is their problem. Their money isn't your problem. So if they come around to you and say that it seems very expensive or it seems like it's a lot of money, you agree with them.

Yes it is expensive. Yeah it is a lot of money. Sign here. Give us the deposit.

Don't they want to get straight to the price?

What if they ask "just tell me the price"? This can throw you off if you weren't expecting it. It's a bit like someone asking "do they die?" when you show someone your favourite movie. You don't want to spoil it! Can't people just be patient?!

The short answer is that we're going to agree with them. We are going to show them the price and they can mull over it all they want. But we're not going to show it to them just yet. The reason is that the customer is desperate to see the price because they want to frame the presentation and project in a term that they can understand. At the moment, they don't have enough information to fully understand the project.

They crave a piece of information that feels like something they can make sense of. It's critical that we don't cave in to this just yet. When the customer is asking to see the price, what they're really saying is "help me understand this more", which is why we spend such a big part of the proposal and pitch repeating back to them words and phrases they've already said. The more they recognise parts of the pitch the more they'll understand. It sounds patronising, maybe even childish, but it's just responding to how the brain works. A bit like I used the analogy of spoiling who dies in a movie, we're going to reframe the pitch into something they do understand. So it's critical that we don't just tell them the price until they fully understand the pitch AND by following this pitch process, they will understand more.

What I respond with when they ask to see the price upfront is "I'll absolutely get to the price and I've got a copy of the proposal to give you to read over. However, I just want to make sure I've understood all aspects of the project and that you agree with what we're proposing so that I can give my most accurate price."

We're framing the call as asking the customer a few more questions and getting their feedback. We want to make sure that we've understood the project and their business and then we'll give a price. If they're persistent (it can happen but it's rare), you can ask "You want the most accurate and best price right, Mr. Customer?" Of course they do, so when they say yes, just respond with "Just let me ask a couple more questions and I'll send the pricing over."

Still no sale or no live call

Occasionally, if someone insists on taking the time to read the proposal or if you never get a chance to get a live meeting with them, I'll still send them the proposal. However, I follow up with a very specific follow up method which massively improved our close rates. Following up in general is critical for most contracts to close anyway. But this first follow up method that I use is so powerful I can't believe more people don't use it. I create a video of the proposal talking through the high level points and give a strong clear call to action at the end.

I'll use Loom or Camtasia or any other screen capture software to record the screen of me going through the proposal. I'll talk over the main points and keep the video to around 5 minutes. Any longer and it's unlikely to be viewed in full. No need to appear on camera or make it look too fancy, just stick to the proposal format and talk over the bullet points with each page on screen.

This video follow up technique alone has landed us sales that we might have lost. I know that many people don't believe in proposals at all and I totally see their point of view. Ideally, a customer that trusts you doesn't need a proposal at all. However, I have found them to be very useful tools for getting a customer over the line. Following up with video is a fantastic way to close a proposal that you might have missed otherwise.

Leading up

"The fortune is in the follow up!"

Dan Kennedy

This final section in this final chapter could be the most important part of the whole book. It's placed here at the end of the book because it is the final stage in getting people over the line. But it's also at the end because of ALL the techniques, stages and templates in this book, *leading up* is the most powerful you can learn. You probably call this process 'following up' and there is absolutely nothing wrong with that. I'll explain the term 'leading up' in a bit and the difference between the two.

I also placed it at the end because I want you to work backwards from following up. Everything else in this book will follow a certain sequence (audience before amount and amount before asset etc.). But following up is something you can implement right now.

As with other tactics and strategies in the book, they are very iterative and evolutionary. Your niche might reveal itself to you over time. You'll tweak the price and deliverables of your products but following up can have an immediate impact on your business, today. Plus, as the rest of your business grows and evolves, following up will become more powerful as you grow. It's something that is a truly future proof concept if you can understand it and use it today.

Following up does not mean 'chasing'

This is a common mistake that many businesses make. Both in terms of execution and understanding. Chasing a customer is when they have something of value that you want. You're chasing them to give you something, therefore they have something of high value. People chase things they can't get and it often makes you look desperate.

The reason I call this process 'leading up' is very simply because the mindset is that we are leading the customer to a better future. WE have the thing they desire. If they chase us, we have something of desire and they 'follow up' with us.

Meanwhile we're 'leading up' and leading our customers to the better, brighter future which they deserve. If you still want to call it 'follow up', I'm not going to argue with you. It's only a dumb change in words to try and frame the mindset around getting the customer onto your product. But for the rest of this section I'm going to refer to the process as 'leading up'.

Imagine you had a member of staff really keen to learn a new skill like copywriting. They've displayed some interest in the past and you think they'd benefit from this new skill. You also believe that your business, team and projects would benefit from them learning this new skill. As their leader, they have approached you asking to better themselves.

You make some calls, get a programme together and are now looking for the staff member to confirm their dates and time and start their training. If they are busy or have stuff to do, or if they take some time off and come back a week later, do you a) chase them or b) lead them? The question is 'do you follow their direction and timescales, or do they follow yours?' The answer of course is b) lead them. They are your member of staff and in your team. With all the best will in the world, people forget stuff and life happens. But *you* know that life is better for them and you if they take this training. So we lead them towards action, rather than just reminding them.

There are three levels of this type of communication, starting with the weakest, 'chasing', which we've talked about. Then 'follow up', which is better but lacks a specific angle. Then 'leading up', the strongest of the styles. Some examples of chasing might be:

"Hey Mike, I was wondering if you saw the times for the training?" or "did you get a chance to read over the programme?"

It's leaving the ball in their court and assuming that the reader will get the hint. This type of chasing is based around the idea that we don't want to put pressure on people or force them into a decision. It's weak, ineffective and tells them that you value being liked by them, more than helping them.

Follow up emails or communication might look like this:

"Hey Mike, just a reminder that your contract is ready to go here" or "Remember to sign your project proposal here and we can get started!"

These are much better and are beginning to give direction to the reader. They're telling them what to do or at least reminding them of what they need to do next.

Finally, leading up looks like this:

"Hey Mike, I want to make sure our team has the bandwidth to start your project. I need you to sign here and send over the deposit and we can get started today."

Specific, clear and we're taking charge. If this was our staff member we'd be telling them that the dates have been set and they need to book some time to do the work. Your customers are looking for someone to take charge and direct them to the best option.

Again, as with the pitch, assume the sale. Assume they want the project to start. Assume your customer wants to work with you and buy. Assume that they are like the staff member that wants to do the training. Assume the sale.

You're missing 92% of sales

There's a reason that car adverts run twice an hour every hour for an entire month. There's a reason your phone continues to ring even when you have heard it. There's a reason that Facebook and YouTube allow specific 'times per view' settings for adverts to an audience. You need to hear and see something multiple times for it to sink in. Google calls this the Zero Moment of Truth and they have some amazing data on the subject. Namely, the business that follows up with the customer the most times, wins.

If you speak to a customer 7 times, and your competition speaks to them 8 times, it's more likely they'll go with the competitor. "7 times!" I hear you exclaim. "Who speaks to a customer 7 times?" Businesses that win! There's an old adage in sales 'if you're not the first person to talk to the customer, you better be the last.' It means that if you don't win the sale on the first call, you better make sure the last person they speak to is you. Because there is no second place in a sale. You either make it or you don't. How many times do you need to talk to the customer? Probably at least 7 times. 7 follow up communications.

Let's say you send a proposal and they don't buy there and then. Bummer. No big deal but now what? Now, you have to follow up. How many times do you follow up? You follow up until they buy or tell you to go away. And if you're leading the customer, because you're leading up, you're leading them until they quit. Most funnel businesses will send 2 or maybe 3 emails asking if the customer is still interested. Then they'll quit and move on. This is what will kill your business. You must follow up and continue to follow up until the customer either buys, or tells you to go away.

"Isn't that pressure selling?" Frankly, applying pressure is important and the customer wants you to pressure them. Sounds controversial, but they do.

Pressure is what causes people to make decisions. If you need to be told not to lie, coerce, manipulate or apply hard sell tactics, then you won't have a business for long anyway. I'm assuming that if you're reading this, you can tell the difference between urgency/pressure and straight up lying. Don't use your fear of offending someone as an excuse to quit the sale early.

Remember, you're LEADING the customer. You're leading them to the future and sometimes that requires a little pressure. The whole 'let the customer take control and be their friend' thing is bullshit when you need someone to take action. Do not mistake the 4% (on average) of people who are ready to buy, with zero leading up, there and then, as indicative of how people buy. The other 96% will need some kind of leading up.

Even motivated and disciplined people need a nudge and a reminder why they're buying. If someone buys there and then, great! But that is the exception, not the rule. That only accounts for 4% of your sales. Other people will buy after 1 or 2 follow ups. Around 4% again.

92% of your sales are waiting to buy and be sold to, after a solid and lengthy leading up process. In fact, as I mentioned, it's probably around 8 times before they pull the trigger. Take the number of sales you made last year and divide it by 8. If you made 2 sales, divided by 8 is 0.25. Multiple that by 100 and that's 25. You missed out on 92% of your potential sales because you didn't follow up. That's 22 potential customers who were already talking to you.

We lead busy lives and forget stuff. You are not the centre of their world. Even customers that want to buy hesitate or forget and need a little nudge. The key is to lead them to the close which we've talked about above. What is the next step that the customer needs to take in order to start benefiting?

A signed document and a deposit? Great! Then get them to do that. And remember, people who haven't bought yet aren't saying "no", they just haven't been lead to the end of that journey. Keep pushing and reminding them, keep leading them. Leading a group of people is hard work but it pays off. As a rule, I tend to follow up using the following timescale:

- Day 0: Close. If not, then lead up later.
- Day 1: Email
- Day 2: Email
- Day 3: Email
- Day 5: Book call
- Day 7: Email
- Day 10: Email
- Day 14: Email
- Day 20: Book call

The emails might share content or attempt a close. Don't worry too much about the content right now, it's more about keeping you top of mind with your customers. The reality is that a customer is more likely to buy immediately after the pitch. Even with all the usual bullshit and excuses about needing time to think it over, or show it to their boss or whatever else, they are never more likely to buy than when you've just sold it to them.

Every hour past that, the customer loses interest and their heat dies down. Their desire to work with you does NOT get stronger the longer you leave it. You categorically must lead up with them and repeatedly close them.

Here's an example email.

Hey Mike
Just doing some research before the project. One of my team is particularly excited about the opportunity with 'email resends'.
Automatically resending a sales campaign to people who didn't open. Looks to be a 2-5x return.
We can get started today, we just need a signature here and then a deposit.

Use your emails to send content, insights, disruptive ideas and of course, closes. Appear keen to take the project on. Be hungry and 'in a hurry to help'. The clearer your enthusiasm for the project and the customer shining through, the more likely they are to buy.

Summary

- Sales is a transference of enthusiasm. If you're excited and enthusiastic about your customers, their lives and their businesses and your product, you'll make sales
- Closing a customer is usually as simple as asking for the deal - don't overcomplicate it
- The customer literally starts benefiting as soon as they give you money. They're not going to say no or get angry, they want you to help them
- Your customers deserve to work with you

FIVE FIGURE FUNNELS

Stripping everything else away, you'll always do well if you focus on selling and closing before anything else. Yes, a niche and content and a process will make life infinitely easier. But most businesses don't work on their sales and closes. If you're looking for a competitive advantage in the marketplace, you can't go wrong with working on your sales.

Admin, accounts, bookkeeping, brand, choosing the best tools, having the fastest website. All of these are great, but absolutely no business in history has even been celebrated for having "really good filing systems". All your goals and dreams and whatever you're working towards will only come true if your business makes sales.

The goal of this book is to make £25,000 sales easier or at least, more accessible. I categorically believe that you are absolutely not special (bear with me here) and that you do not need to be special. There is infinite value in who you are NOW, without needing special treatment or be treated differently for who you are. I don't believe that anyone is special but that everyone *is* capable of massive contribution to communities and society.

Try not to think of payment and money as rewards or compensation for your value. Think of it instead as a tool to accelerate your contributions and solve larger problems. Self-reliance is an important ideal to both myself and Sell Your Service. The more we can become self-reliant, the more we can give back and help others.

Start with your audience. The people you're going to work with and what problems they're facing. What are they looking to transform into? Who are they now? What do they not like about their life and what do they want in their life? So many businesses immediately go to the products and services they can build, hoping that if it's interesting or exciting enough they'll find a market. The story of the inventor who could never sell anything is so commonplace it's practically a stereotype. Similarly, the inventor who has genuinely good ideas but never makes a difference because they never get that idea to market, is also a lesson from history that people forget.

Next work on your amount or pricing. It's *your* pricing. No one else's. They don't know your margins or costs or goals. Your competition, customers and colleagues should have zero influence over your price because you'll be picking the price first and then working out what you're going to deliver.

Those deliverables are called assets. Both in terms of the process you'll be following, but also the benefits to the customer that they'll experience once they've bought. Again so many funnel builders and marketing agencies refuse to move away from the definition of what they do. That's like the architect talking non-stop about how good they are at drawing blueprints and building ideas without ever asking me what I want to build. I don't want blueprints, I want a house I can live in. Don't confuse a deep understanding of what you do with expertise. Your customers do not care about the minutiae of your process, they care about their life. This is often where people get confused about the role of education in sales. Thinking that someone buys because they're educated enough about your product and how it works is a dangerous assumption. They're buying because they believe their life will be better and they understand how it impacts their future. Sell futures, not features.

Your authority in the industry will be directly proportional to the amount of content you produce. It really is that simple. The crazy thing is that authority can be created from nothing, for free, with just the investment of time. Even if you *are* the best in the world at something, it means nothing to the customer unless you're telling people about it. Remember, you're not special. But you have infinite value and if you feel you could do more with that value, then let people see it.

And through the creation of authority, you attract attention. The process of people noticing you, what you do and how you can help them. Realistically, every single person in this book should be able to generate referrals and sales within a few days. What stops every single person from doing and achieving that is the fear of being disliked. Worrying that someone somewhere will think "less" of you because of reaching out. I hear excuse after excuse about why some people can't generate referrals and sales from starting out. "I don't have a list, I'm not you, I don't have experience" and when you boil it down, it's a fear of being disliked. That irrational and misplaced fear is literally the only thing standing in your way of emailing people and getting on calls.

Finally, we take action and close the attention you've been building. I could talk for hours on closing and asking for the deal. But as we've already seen, most businesses don't fail to make the sale because they have a bad product or because they're not good at sales. They fail to get the deal because they don't tell people what the next step is.

I just need a deposit and a signature here and we can get started today. Simple as that. Most of your deals will be won because you use that closing sentence. Yes, some people will say no, or give you a reason not to buy, or ask a question. But almost every single one of them will buy eventually because you (or someone else) made it clear what the next steps are.

This book is really the first book I should have written and published. My other books were fun and have yielded great attention in the market. But haven't been specific to the mission for Sell Your Service. Help more funnel builders sell marketing funnels.

It's also been a journey to get the book written and published. 2020 has been a hell of a year for many people. And my family suffered a sudden and heart-breaking loss just as we started the year. But for every moment of doubt and lack of motivation, I knew that there will be some people reading this who will take control and attack the opportunity. They'll see this book more as permission to get started and they'll go further than I could have expected. It's my hope that you are one of those people. I want *you* to write the next book Seven Figure Funnels and teach me how to sell marketing services for £1 million.

If you have any questions, please just email me michael@sellyourservice.co.uk or head to sellyourservice.co.uk and let's get in touch.

Have courage, commit, take action.

Mike

ABOUT THE AUTHOR

Michael Killen is the founder of Sell Your Service. He gives marketing funnel agencies the confidence to create multiple scalable streams of income, to free them from the crushing constraints of the traditional out-dated agency model.

Mike is the bestselling author of From Single To Scale and Universe Fuel. He believes that most people don't live the life they want or deserve is down to a lack of confidence. Long term his goal is to get confidence training in school curricula.

Made in the USA
Las Vegas, NV
04 January 2023

64971040R00111